Rock Scissors Paper

Understanding How Environment Affects
Your Performance on a Daily Basis

Debbie Bowie, MA, MS

This book was edited and shepherded by Dianne Morr at Morr Creative Writing Services, www.morrcreative.com.

For information contact:
Debbie Bowie
Rock Scissors Paper Institute
804-730-4991
debbie@rockscissorspaperinstitute.com

Contents

Acknowledgments

For years I had been urged to write a book by clients and friends who enjoyed hearing the stories about my work. I wanted to write a book and knew I was supposed to write one, but the task seemed so daunting. I even began writing the stories of particularly memorable client experiences that taught me very important lessons. But then I got stuck. Perhaps I remembered the emotional challenge of writing my master's thesis, with its accompanying meltdown and knew that I didn't want to go there again.

Organizers break big tasks into small parts and gradually move mountains of clutter and chaos to create order. I could do that for others, but my mountain of stories and ideas and information that I wanted to share seemed insurmountable until I heard Dan Poynter, the guru of self-publishing. He recommended "blooking," writing blog entries over time and combining them into a book. What a great idea! I took that idea and filed it away until I could figure out how to make myself write on a regular basis. Thanks, so much, Dan.

Mark LeBlanc planted the seed that got me writing every day. I came away from his Achiever's Circle in Nashville, Tennessee in

June of 2008 committed to do three high value activities every day that would move my business forward. One of my high value activities each day was to write a few paragraphs, client success stories and lessons I'd learned from clients. That discipline led me to create a collection of stories, many of which are included in this book.

About a year later I asked Mark to be my coach. In our first session he told me, "I want you to write a book in 90 days. You'll call it 'Understanding How Environment Affects Your Performance on a Daily Basis.'"

After taking several deep breaths I asked, "And, how do I do that?"

"Write 50 minutes five days a week," he replied.

"Ok, I can do that," I said with fear and trembling.

One of the reasons I had been struggling with writing this book was that I could not figure out how to organize it. In that same conversation with Mark I asked him if I could use "rock scissors paper" in the title, as I had been urged to do by Sam Horn, the consultant who helped rename my company and work on a name for my book. After learning that "rock scissors paper" is a cryptic way to state the primary clutter clearing method I recommend, he said, "Sure! And, your book will have three parts: rock, scissors and paper." With that recommendation the organization of the book fell into place. Using those words as my guide, I was off and running.

So, thank you, Sam and Dan for great ideas that gave me a vision and a method for what I could do. And, Mark, were it not for your exquisite wisdom, your ability to distill complex ideas and desires into a manageable project, and your setting a deadline to aim for, I'd still be stuck trying to figure out how move forward. You also made aspects of this project easier by sending me to my editor, Dianne Morr, my cover designer, Joni McPherson, and my printer, SPS Publications. You gave me information and guidance that removed all the barriers to making this book come to life in 2009. Knowing that you believed I could do it was the foundation I returned to time and again when my energies waned, my belief in myself wobbled or the whole project seemed too big. Your support was invaluable.

Joni McPherson deserves kudos for taking my content and expressing its essence in the design of the book cover. Thank you for your patience with this feng shui practitioner who had to have everything "feel" good, from the colors to the font to the images.

Dianne Morr was not only my editor, but a cheerleader and gentle source of support as we worked together to take my words and ideas and present them in the best order and the best light. She too was patient beyond belief with my need to make this book something people would want to pick up and read both for its content and for the look and feel of it. Thank you for taking this journey with me, Dianne.

Another source of support standing solidly behind me as I moved from talking about writing this book to getting it published was my mastermind group, Vision Quest. Cara Kinning, Dave Prestia, Fiona Marissa, Coleen Kenny, Carrie Williar, Geena Lockett, Ivan Alzuro, and Josh Baldwin have all held the space for the success of this project. They showed up week after week to hold me accountable for the many tasks necessary to make this dream a reality. Thank you, my dear friends.

Frank Fife, my surrogate father, and my mother, Lyn Arrix, both believed I could do anything I set my mind to do. Their belief in me has made me who I am today, an empowered woman capable of writing a book and much more. My father, Russ Randall, appreciated my creative abilities and passed on his gift for writing. What a gift that is!

And, finally, I thank my husband, Bob, for taking several difficult leaps of faith to see this project through with me. I can't thank him enough for hanging in there through the lonely times when I'd be off writing, for always being a willing editor, and for keeping me laughing.

Introduction

In 2008 I spoke to interior design students at West Virginia University on Clearing Clutter to Improve Outcome. My speech was scheduled mid-day in a long rectangular room in the basement of an old college building. The walls were painted white. Exposed pipes and fluorescent light fixtures hung above our heads. The only place for me to stand was right in front of the only door to the room. Late students had to edge around me to take their seats. Students sat in desks of a nondescript color. Windows were set high in the wall on one side of the room.

Rock Scissors Paper

The atmosphere of the room was as gray and lifeless as the color scheme. Even the students looked colorless and lacked energy.

As I prepared to speak I remember feeling sluggish, as if I couldn't get my engine running. I knew my content was good. Most people get very enthusiastic about clearing clutter once they realize how it is affecting their performance and their outcomes. I just couldn't access my own energy and inspiration.

I trudged through the speech; answered a few good questions and received some good comments following it. But I felt disappointed about my performance.

If I feel disappointed about my performance when I speak, I evaluate my situation to try to make sense of what happened. I figured out that these factors were not working in my favor:

- The walls were painted white. I felt as if I was talking in a snow storm or a deep fog. Color doesn't attach to white. We need color to nurture us and add energy to spaces. My speech required me to be inspiring in an energy desert.
- The basement location added another challenge. Natural energies are lower in a basement than anywhere else in a building.

- Fluorescent lighting gives a harsh light that stresses the nervous system and drains energy.
- Standing in front of the doorway put me right in the middle of the energy flow into the room. Our brains work best when we have a solid wall behind us and a full view in front of us, the power position. I did not have a solid wall behind me. In addition, people entered the room behind me, distracting me from my message. My nervous system was on high alert. I couldn't completely focus on my speech.

A Better Presentation

By contrast, I spoke on the same topic to a group of 50 professional women. I presented the second speech at an event sponsored by Virginia Asset Management, LLC, a financial services company. In this case the carefully planned event provided an environment that complemented the content of my speech.

We met in a country club ballroom with a high ceiling and stately columns around the perimeter. Incandescent lighting flooded the ballroom and natural light shone through large windows opening onto a green lawn. The yellow wall color provided a warm backdrop. Comfortable burgundy chairs lined up facing the podium.

Asian food had been prepared in a room off the primary space, so the appealing aroma of garlic and cooking meat and vegetables greeted people as they arrived. Fresh flowers, fruits and vegetables added color and healthy nourishment. I spoke from the right side of the room with a solid wall behind me. I also had a full view of the participants and the door.

This speech was the best speech I had EVER given! When I again evaluated the situation looking for an explanation for my results, I discovered that every factor was in my favor.

- The room was warm, welcoming and well lit.
- Comfortable, nourishing color from many sources set the tone for the event.
- The space was lovely – large enough to accommodate the size of the audience, but with an intimate feel created by the wall color and layout of the room.
- I spoke from an empowered position with a solid wall behind me and a full view in front of me.

Two Speeches ~ Two Outcomes

What made the difference? Two entirely different environments. Granted, other factors in addition to environment, such as audience energy and age, my energy and mindset, and time of day affected the meeting. But, when I think back to those two experiences, what stands out in my mind is the feel of each environment.

The West Virginia University classroom felt cool, impersonal and uninviting. Consequently I felt like a stranger in a foreign land, stressed with a brain that was on overdrive, preoccupied with finding comfort and safety.

The Virginia Asset Management ballroom felt warm and inviting. All my senses were pleasantly stimulated. I was able to speak feeling personally empowered and utterly safe, with no distractions to disturb me.

The outcomes of both speeches? I received positive comments from members of both audiences. Testimonials indicated that people from both audiences had taken action as a result of hearing me speak. But far more participants from the second event interacted with me.

I have no doubt that my performance for the Virginia Asset Management speech far exceeded that of the West Virginia University speech.

The level of comfort you feel in a space affects what you do in that space. Environment affects performance on a daily basis. Learning what affects your performance and working to create environments that make it possible for the best you to be present can move you to greater empowerment and happiness.

Love It, Use It or Lose It!™

You will find these words recurring throughout this book. They are a guiding principle of my life and my work. They are key to creating and maintaining a high performance environment. When you live exclusively with what you love or use, and release things that you don't love or use, your living and working environments feel good. The environment nurtures and supports you, and you thrive.

Rock Scissors Paper

Rock Scissors Paper stands for Love It, Use It or Lose It™. Rocks are **loved** for their comforting, grounding energy. Scissors can be **used** to cut things, and paper is something you want to **lose** to keep your life and your performance moving and sane.

This book is arranged in three Parts: Rock, Scissors and Paper. High performance environments are a reflection of the Love It, Use It or Lose It™ principle.

The first part describes the "rocks," the principles of high performance environments. When you apply those principles to your space, you will love the results. Over time you will come to love using them as a reliable guide whenever you need to ground yourself and want to work toward specific results.

Part two describes the "scissors," specific tools that can create high performance environments. Using effective tools helps you to get more of what you really want.

Part three, "paper," gives instructions on how to lose those things like paper that negatively affect performance, the first step toward creating a high energy, high performance environment.

I am confident that you will find that as you apply the principles of Rock Scissors Paper, you will see your energy, comfort and productivity skyrocket.

Part I

Rock

"You are here to enable the divine purpose of the universe to unfold. That is how important you are."

Ekhardt Tolle

Have you ever walked into a room and felt an immediate urge to back out of it because you felt so uncomfortable? By contrast, recall a time when you walked into a room and felt like you wanted to settle in and stay forever because it was lovely and comfortable. What was the difference between those two environments? What had such a profound effect on your comfort level and your willingness to stay in a space?

The principles introduced in Part I will help you understand what you experience in different environments. Understanding these principles helps you create spaces where you can access your genius and thrive.

Chapter One

Energy

Everything in your space is energy. Everything. From the papers in your files to the photographs on your desk to the quality of light in the room. Everything is energy. The quality of those energies has a profound effect on how you perform in that area.

Martin Miller, a financial advisor with Scott & Stringfellow, gave me permission to share his story. I want to give you a concrete example of what can happen if you commit yourself to treating your home or office environment with the same commitment you might treat your body and your physical health.

Rock

I have known Martin for nine years and during that time, Martin has moved his office five times. He began in a small space where the options for making improvements to his working environment were limited to clearing out "dead" papers from his files and setting up a desktop system for optimal work flow. His space was so small there was little he could do to improve it with color, lights and bringing the outdoors inside. But, Martin, who is conscientious and self-disciplined, took my recommendations to heart and worked hard to control what he could, especially the influx of paper. He was rewarded by being moved to a better location in the office.

Each time Martin moved to a new office he hired me to set up his new space. When he landed in an office with walls and windows, we had more to work with. His desk was placed in the power position. We carefully arranged his furniture so he could get things done efficiently. We placed art and added lighting and plants in strategic positions.

Each move gave us the opportunity to clear out old papers that had accumulated. Financial advisors work with quantities of papers that go out of date more quickly than they have time to purge them. Moving was actually a benefit for Martin because it caused him to go through all his papers every couple of years.

From the first time I worked with Martin he really understood that the condition of his environment had an effect on his performance, his productivity and his bottom line. In between moves he worked hard to maintain his office as a clutter-free zone. When I asked him recently how much clutter he has in his space he replied, "Zero clutter." He leaves his desk clear of papers each night and returns to work organized and ready to get to work.

"I can't control the market. I can only control my actions," he said. "I am my pension. If I want to reach my goals I need to have systems in place. My office is the space where I earn my living. It must be a place I feel good about so I can be productive. I can't work in a disorganized space. I have to have order to keep up with the work flow. I am very disciplined about maintaining my space and prioritizing all day, every day, regardless of daily distractions."

You may be wondering what effect Martin's space and his commitment to maintaining an organized, lovely space has had on his productivity. Since 2000 the market has had two significant downturns, from 2000 to 2003 and from 2008 to 2009. Martin's income has increased every year despite significant fluctuations in the market. **He is currently making four times what he was making in 2000.** He has increased the number of clients every year. And, he has increased the number of assets under management every year through 2008. Even in the worst year in the history of the market since the Great Depression, 2008, his gross production increased 5.2%. Martin is in the top third of brokers at Scott & Stringfellow in gross production. Most of the brokers in the top third have been in business much longer than he has, in some cases decades longer.

Martin believes his commitment to maintaining a space that looks good, feels good, and is clutter free and organized is as important as his being disciplined about seeking new clients and managing existing accounts. Even in the most challenging economic times, the order and comfort and solid systems in his office supported growth in his business.

The Quality of Energy

The energy of a particular object is determined by these variables:

- Age
- Associations
- Condition
- Previous owner
- How it makes you feel

Age

Age can increase or decrease the energy of a particular object. Papers of a particular project tend to lose positive energy over time unless they are key documents that are used often as references. Books, for example, can become outdated and lose positive energy or can become prized possessions because they are favorite, timeless references.

Associations

Objects associated with a positive memory, person, or project have positive energies. Those that remind you of a difficult time or person have negative energies. Some things have no clear association.

For example, a file that holds information about a prospect with whom you were unsuccessful perhaps holds the energy of frustration and failure. A diploma of a completed college degree holds the energy of success.

“I can't work at my desk when there are papers all over it!” said Mary, a client of many years. As I sat there looking at her tiny computer desk with papers strewn about, I could understand that.

Once again Mary was stuck. This was not an unusual occurrence, but on this particular day there were not many papers on her desk compared to other times. I had a hunch there was something else going on besides shutdown due to the negative energy of the papers.

As we sorted through the papers I paid close attention to the content they held. Mary is very sensitive to the emotional content of things. I knew that even one item that reminded her of a difficult time in her past could stop her cold.

In fact there was one letter that required she make a name change from that of her deceased husband to her own name. Anything that held her husband's energy could have a powerful effect on Mary. But, her reaction to this letter was minor.

As we were working I noticed that I could feel the weight of stacks of piled projects and papers on a table to the right of us. When I mentioned this to Mary, she immediately pointed to a large manuscript. "That's my thesis!" She wanted to send it to several universities and it was waiting there as a reminder for her to take the necessary steps. Though the task seemed ominous to Mary, that task also did not hold enough negative energy to shut her down. However, the thesis was done during a period of high stress and difficulty in her family. It held the energy of that time, and it was a very powerful energy.

I suggested that we write the task on a sticky note, add it to her list of things to do later, and put the thesis out of sight. Mary agreed. We made the note and filed the thesis. Immediately Mary's mood shifted and lifted.

Condition

Spaces and objects that are in good condition have positive energies. Those that are broken, damaged, worn or soiled have negative energies. Sometimes we don't notice that our possessions deteriorate with age. It helps to consciously take a look at our space from time to time as if we are seeing it for the first time.

Previous Owner

Spaces and items that once belonged to someone else hold the energy of that person. If that person was successful, they hold the energy of success. If that person was unsuccessful, they hold the energy of failure. For example, the office of a broker who struggled to keep his head above water holds the energy of struggle. The energy of that broker affected everything in that space. If the occupant had been a hardworking success, the office would hold the energy of success.

How It Makes You Feel

If you pay attention, you will notice that you feel positive or negative feelings all the time in relation to particular objects, people, situations and environments. You are reading their energies. In some cases you may feel neutral, no strong feelings either way. That indicates no real positive feelings and no strong negative feelings. Over time, an accumulation of things about which you feel nothing tend to develop a negative energy.

Some items hold mixed energies. For example, your career may require that you complete a task you really don't enjoy doing. A file associated with that task may have a negative, annoying energy. But, the instruction manual in the file may be helpful to you and hold a positive energy.

The best way to determine the energy of anything is to pay attention to how you feel. Things that have positive energy lift your spirits, make your heart smile, or energize you. Things that have negative energy cause your spirit to dip; they feel heavy and burdensome. It is fairly common to feel a knot in your stomach when dealing with things that have negative energy.

Energy Talks to You

Not only is everything energy, the energy talks to you. That's why it's so hard to work or think clearly in a room full of clutter. The energy of everything in the room is talking to you at once. Dozens of conversations are going on at the same time! When you look at items in your space, thoughts flow through your mind. For example, a pile of unprocessed paper might say, "Oh, boy, you are behind. There's probably something important you are forgetting." Another might say, "What is wrong with you that you can't keep up with these papers?" Everything talks.

So, it makes sense that the more objects you have in a space, the more conversations you have. Even if neatly organized, a room packed with too many items sounds and feels like a roaring crowd – very distracting and very tiring. Add disorder to a packed room and you feel like you are being exposed to the energy of a riot. You feel overwhelmed and likely want to run away. The price you pay if you spend time in a messy, busy environment is to be drained of energy.

It's really a double bind. You need energy to address the problems in your space. But, the condition of the space drains you of energy.

Let me give you an example. Have you ever been determined to get something done but found the space so confusing that you were unable to think straight? That happened to me one day when I was working at a client's apartment.

There were so many piles of mixed paper in that room that my brain just froze. After taking a deep breath to center myself, I identified the cause of my shutdown. I remembered that everything is energy and that energy talks to you all the time. All the conversations going on around me were the culprit.

In that room filled with piles of paper there were hundreds, perhaps thousands of conversations going on at the same time. Every time I tried to get started in one direction, I kept getting distracted by chatter in another direction. Aargh!!!!!

I had to remind myself what works in those fuzzy moments when too many conversations freeze my brain. Start with the big stuff! So, that's what I did.

I forced myself to keep pushing all the individual pieces of paper aside, and instead chose to focus on the big bags of mixed items that littered the floor around my client's chair. Several of the bags just needed to be unpacked and their contents put away in other parts of the apartment. After I did that, I could see the floor. Just that much clarity helped me get a grip on the clutter and begin to sort the paper in a productive way. Whew! The paper was still pretty overwhelming, but I was no longer stuck!

Your Space Reflects Your Current Self

Your space is a reflection of your current consciousness. The spaces you occupy are an outer expression of your inner self. Do you like what you see? Does your space reflect a happy, productive, successful person? Or, does it reflect an overwhelmed, exhausted, stressed person?

If you don't like what you see, change it. Changing your environment can change your consciousness.

Predecessor Energy

Remember, even though spaces are a reflection of your current self, the spaces are also affected by the energies of previous occupants, as mentioned in the example of the broker. If the previous occupant of your home or office had many financial challenges, that person left behind the energy of financial challenges. If you occupy that space without doing something to clear those negative energies, they will affect you. You are more likely to experience similar financial struggles in that environment.

Performing a space clearing is a good idea when you move into a space that was previously occupied by someone else – especially when you are aware that the previous occupant had struggles of any kind.

A common method of space clearing is to burn dried sage as you walk the perimeter of a space, starting and ending at the primary entrance to the room. Other methods such as ringing bells and flicking water throughout the space are discussed in detail in Karen Kingston's *Creating Sacred Space with Feng Shui*, a good guide for space clearing.

Individual objects, as well as spaces, hold the energy of previous owners or of the person who gave them to you. Because objects hold the energy of people associated with them, it is as if those people are in the room with you. Once you become conscious of that fact, you can make choices about whose energy you want to have around you.

As you might expect, past projects and papers from previous occupants hold the energies of both the outcomes of the projects and the people associated with those projects. Their energies can be distracting and can affect current outcomes.

"Oh, you're the woman who changed my life!" I heard when I answered the phone. At the other end of the phone line was the husband of a woman who had recently attended one of my speeches.

Clearing my throat I asked tentatively, "What exactly did I do?"

"You told my wife to get rid of everything that belonged to my mother!" Before I could respond he continued with, "And, that was a really good thing because we've been feuding with her for years!"

Whew! That was good news! Not that he and his mother had problems. Rather, it was good news that my advice had helped this man and his wife instead of causing them problems.

The husband's mother had given this couple several pieces of furniture. The furniture therefore was associated with her and held her energy. It occupied prime space in their dining room that they used every day. It was like having Mom sitting down to eat with them at every meal. Her energy and the feelings of anger or loss about the relationship were in their face every day.

This man felt grateful for being released from the tyranny of the negative energy associated with his mother.

Clearing out his mother's things started the couple on a positive path. They moved on to de-clutter the whole house and garage. Within a couple of years they were able to move to a much nicer house in a much more desirable neighborhood. It's possible that his mother's energy, held in place by her furnishings, was the block that had kept them stuck in that smaller house.

Martin's income has increased every year despite significant fluctuations in the market. He is currently making four times what he was making in 2000.

Chapter Two

Energy Affects Outcome

The furnishings and materials in your space and how they are arranged affect what happens in that space. Like energies are attracted to each other. Positive energy attracts more positive energy. Negative energy attracts more negative energy.

You can easily see this principle play out in your relationships. If you speak to another person in anger, the knee-jerk response of that person is to respond in anger. So too in your physical space, a negative energy source – like clutter – attracts more clutter. Isn't it amazing how one small pile of paper can mushroom into multiple piles? It's as if the original source of negative energy gives the whole space permission to be cluttered.

If your home or office is neat, organized, comfortable and functional, you are likely to attract positive experiences and to handle any challenges with confidence and success. If your home or office is crammed with decades worth of old papers, is in disarray and is anything but inviting; you are more likely to attract challenges and obstacles to your progress. You may feel burdened and distracted, and find it hard to work efficiently. Being productive will be hard won and come at a steep price.

Once you understand this principle and become conscious of sources of negative energy, you can quickly eliminate sources of negative energy and restore positive energy. You will find yourself becoming more and more committed to maintaining positive energy because you know you will attract more and more positive people and experiences into your life.

The Importance of Intention

Understanding that like energies are attracted to each other, you can intentionally set up spaces to attract what you really want. For example, if you want prosperity and fulfilling relationships, you can create a space that reflects those desires.

What do you really want? Set your intention and then express that intention in your space. Getting clear about what you really want is the first step toward getting it. Keep that intention in the forefront of your mind as you work to create a space that is congruent with your intention. Then, maintain the space and watch for results.

"Are you involved in a relationship?" I asked Betty. "No, but I'd like to be," she replied.

I was looking at her large bedroom that seemed to attract all kinds of clutter just because there was room for it. Bedrooms are spaces associated with relationships and intimacy, and her bedroom was not likely to attract a relationship.

"What would you think about switching your home office and your bedroom? That would put the bedroom in a smaller, more intimate space at the back of the house where energies are lower and it will be easier to sleep. And, you will have more room in your home office for all the things that have been spilling over into the bedroom."

She enthusiastically agreed to the plan. As we began making the switch I advised her to set her intention for wanting a good, long-term relationship.

Rock

Within several months I again had the opportunity to work with Betty. This time she introduced me to her new boyfriend. And, they later married!

Everything Is Connected

Spaces are a mix of energies, both positive and negative. Nothing exists in isolation. One item with negative energy negatively affects the feel of the whole space.

For example, imagine entering a room that has been thoughtfully and beautifully furnished. Your eyes scan the room, drinking in the comfort and beauty. Then you notice a lamp in one corner of the room with a broken shade. As you look at the lamp you feel a slight discomfort and the pleasure you were just feeling diminishes slightly. The negative energy of that one broken object affected your perception of the whole room.

The goal in creating a high energy, high performance environments is to have mostly positive energy and a minimal amount of negative energy. Negative energies anywhere, even in closets and drawers, have an impact on positive energies and performance.

A participant in one of my seminars told me that she had cleared out a closet in her home. When she finished, she closed the door and went about her day. Upon returning home some time later she noticed that her house felt different. It felt better, lighter. She was amazed that clearing one closet could affect spaces beyond the closet. She said that family members also visited and wondered what she had done to change her home.

When we clear spaces out in the open for all to see, it's easy to understand that everything is connected because it's easy to feel the effect of shifting from negative to positive energies. This story reminds us that shifts from negative to positive energy in places we can't easily see also benefit the whole space because everything is connected!

I had been working with Denise for well over a year to create a functional home office. For several reasons we seemed to tread water, just keeping her head above a sea of papers that relentlessly kept pouring in.

Then one day I arrived to find the addition of several pieces of furniture to her home office. How had that happened? During our previous organizing session, when we tackled tasks that had been haunting Denise for some time, we came across a reminder notice to get her piano tuned.

"I really want to move it upstairs," she said, "but I don't know who I can get to do that."

"Call the piano tuner and ask him," I suggested. She made the call and left a message.

To my surprise and delight, the furniture I found in her office had been moved in preparation for moving the piano. And, that furniture was just what we needed to set up the office to be fully functional.

Sometimes one small action can surprise you! Because everything is connected, one phone call not only led to moving a piano, it also facilitated the creation of an improved work space!

Energy Affects Your Energy

Feeling depleted, I was listening to a lecture about getting more energy. As expected, we took a look at those activities, people and conditions that feed our energy and those that deplete our energy. At the top of the list for energy drainers was a messy environment. I was impressed that this factor had been identified.

The presenter really understood that a messy space is a significant drag on our personal energy.

Why is it that a messy environment sucks our personal energy? As I've mentioned before, everything has energy. The energy of everything runs from positive to negative depending on individual characteristics. When you put things together in a space you get a mix of energies. Objects have energy and the arrangement of the objects has energy.

If **all** the objects and the condition of the space have positive energy, the space feels positive and you feel energized and optimistic in that space. If **most** of the objects and the condition of the space have positive energy, you feel positive, but not quite as positive in that space.

If **many** of the objects have negative energy – for example, they are broken, worn out, or faded – negative energy is likely to dominate. In that case you are more likely to feel listless, distracted and unmotivated, even if the space is perfectly organized.

Let's consider another example. Imagine entering a room filled with many lovely high energy objects in disarray. The objects may have positive energy, but the chaos is negative. You feel stressed and your energy is depleted.

There is an energetic payoff for clearing clutter and getting organized. You feel more energized and are likely to perform at a higher level.

I regularly observe clients become more and more energized as they make decisions to get rid of items they don't love, want or use. The energy often manifests in their posture. They stand straighter as the burden of the negative energy is lifted.

Clients also speak more enthusiastically and rapidly. They begin expressing ideas about everything from how to organize the space we are working in to how to engage family members in the process of organizing.

The energy that was being held by unwanted, unnecessary items is released as the items are removed from the space. Clients gain energy not only from the release of that energy, but also from feeling relieved of the presence of the negative energies associated with stagnation and negative associations.

Everything Is Always Changing

You have only to look in the mirror each day to realize that everything is changing. Or, watch your children grow or the seasons pass. You live in an ever-changing world, and so too your space is always changing. Some people are discomfited by change. "I hate change!" they'll say, not consciously realizing that change is inevitable.

Once you become conscious of the principle of inevitable change, you can make a deliberate choice to embrace change. You can choose to make changes to your living and working environments to coincide with changes in your circumstances and your thinking. Your environment should change as you change.

For example, perhaps you are ready to expand your business by taking on several employees. You realize that in order for employees to be successful, it is best that they feel utterly comfortable in their working environment.

The walls of your space were painted white more than five years ago and they have become dingy. You decide to repaint the walls an attractive sage green, a color that is at once attractive and grounding, but also has the energy of growth and expansion. Because you are ready for the change of growth and expansion, and you realize your space should change as you change, you paint the room. This may be the first step you take to set up a high performance environment.

Characteristics of High Performance Environments

- Clean
- Organized
- Uncluttered
- Walls painted a color, not white
- Good natural lighting—not too bright, not too dim
- Well lit—with at least three sources of incandescent light
- Attractive, comfortable furniture in good condition
- Healthy live plants or clean silk plants
- Interesting, colorful art
- Mementos that are significant to the occupant

Characteristics of Low Performance Environments

- Dusty, dirty
- Disorganized
- Cluttered
- White or gray walls
- Little or no natural light
- Fluorescent lighting only
- Unattractive, uncomfortable or broken furniture
- No plants
- Faded, dated, dull art
- Few or no personal mementos

Your environment should change

as you change.

Part II

Scissors

"Success is not a result of good luck; it's the result of good choices."

Julie Alexander

In Part I you were introduced to the principles that explain why spaces feel and function as they do. The Rock chapters provided a big picture explanation regarding how environment affects performance.

Part II, Scissors, is devoted to identifying the specific tools that can be used to create high energy spaces, spaces of positive energy that feel comfortable and allow you to perform at your best.

Scissors

The tools used to design your spaces include: color, lighting, condition, individual objects, position and views.

Becoming conscious of these tools and their effects on your space will allow you to walk into any space and figure out how to make it feel more comfortable. When feelings of comfort in a space are increased, performance improves.

Each of these tools is significant and is part of the greater whole. Remember, everything is connected.

In my years working with clients in home and office environments, I've found that the tools that seem to have the greatest impact on people, their behavior and mood are color, specifically wall color, and lighting. Effective use of color and lighting can profoundly affect a person's clarity of thought, motivation and mood.

Chapter Three

Color

When you look into your space, are you greeted by a sea of gray and white or are you greeted by a variety of colors? Unfortunately, many office environments are dominated by gray and white because white paint is less expensive than colored paint and has been a standard for years. And, much office equipment is a neutral gray, putty or tan. Gray carpeting has also been a norm because it wears better than other shades.

For years white walls in homes were the norm because they were neutral and gave spaces a fresh clean look. Unfortunately, environments dominated by grays and whites seem impersonal and are uninviting. They have the energy of a cloudy day or a snow storm.

I have heard that white walls are associated with anxiety and depression. Instinctively I knew that was true, but I wondered why. As I became more conscious of the power of color to affect our feelings and the comfort of a space, I realized color feeds our psyche and makes us feel comfortable. Color nurtures us.

In addition, the colors of objects in a room don't show up well in a white environment. A white background can make even interesting furnishings look less attractive.

In a gray/white environment you have to expend your energy to overcome feelings of discomfort before you can get to work. You not only need to find energy to deal with your work, but you also need to find energy to keep yourself from running away to places of greater comfort.

High Energy Colors

The high energy colors are red, green and yellow. Red is associated with fire and has the highest of energies. It should be used sparingly, preferably as an accent rather than a wall color.

Green is associated with the trees, growth and expansion. It is an optimistic color and encourages positive growth.

Yellow is the brightest of the earth tones. It is generally associated with an optimistic, grounded energy. Yellow, because of its association with the sun, the source of the heat and energy coming to earth, is a high energy earth element. The more vibrant the shade of yellow, the more energy it has.

Cool Colors

Black, reminiscent of a deep lake, tends to cool off hot spaces. Blue, like green, is a cool color with a grounding, peaceful energy. Earth tones like browns, tans, taupe and sand are the lowest energy colors, the most restful.

Wall Color

Wall color typically has the greatest effect of any color on the energies of a room because walls are usually the greatest expanses of that one color.

Scissors

If you want to make a space more comfortable and create an environment where particular types of activities are likely to happen, changing the wall color should be the first consideration.

As with everything else, colors have energy. Once you understand the type of energy a color has, you can choose the best color for the function of your space.

The Essential Energy of Common Colors

Red

- Is the highest energy color
- Is best used as an accent color when a pop of energy is needed
- Is not recommended as a wall color unless combined with another color like black or other dark tones that help neutralize its heat
- Can cause feelings of irritability, anger or aggression when used as a wall color in a gathering space like a meeting room, dining room or family room
- Can make sleep difficult if used as a wall color in a bedroom

Green

- Has the energy of growth and expansion
- In a shade of sage, green is recommended as a wall color for offices, particularly men's offices
- Is not recommended as a wall color in bedrooms of couples because it cools off relationships
- Is recommended as a wall color in children's rooms or guest rooms
- Is a good accent color in any room because it brings the feeling of the outdoors inside
- Is an essential accent color in rooms dominated by earth tones

Blue

- Has the energy of growth and expansion though usually calmer than greens
- Is not recommended as a wall color for offices unless used as an accent wall because it is difficult to find a shade that is warm enough for an office
- Is best used as an accent color in wall hangings, chair fabric and decorative items

Yellow

- Has the energy of positive activity
- Is recommended for bathrooms and gathering places like halls, kitchens and women's offices
- In shades other than buttery, yellow can make spaces feel too hot

White

- Has no active energy
- Is best used for ceilings or as an accent
- Makes spaces dominated by blues and greens feel more comfortable

Black

- Has no active energy
- Is best used as an accent
- Makes rooms that have a hot energy, like those with a predominance of reds and yellows, feel more comfortable

Wall Colors for High Performance Environments

High performance rooms require high energy colors in carefully chosen shades. Use high energy colors; toned down shades of red such as terra-cotta, salmon and peach; comfortable shades of green, like sage green; and comfortable shades of yellow with buttery and golden tones.

Avoid hot shades of red because red's energy is so intense that it can be over-stimulating and incite irritability and aggression. Avoid white, shades of white and pastel colors that communicate as white because white environments can feel impersonal, sterile and uninviting. White environments have the energy of inflexibility.

Avoid earth tones, like browns, dark tans, golden tans as wall colors in work spaces, because earth tones have the lowest energies and are not conducive to taking action. Earth tones are best used in break rooms and home environments, places where rest and relaxation is desired.

Touches of Color

While wall color sets the mood and tone for a room, touches of color in wall hangings, fabrics, rugs, decorative items and other objects add small bursts of energy that provide visual interest. These pops of color make a high energy space much more comfortable. ***Comfortable high energy spaces are high performance spaces.***

Even a small splash of a high energy color can transform a room. A room filled with neutral colors, from the wall color to the carpet to the window coverings and decorative items, can be brought to life by the addition of a vase of multi-colored flowers. A healthy green plant on a window sill can add a pop of energy to a drab environment.

One way to better understand the meaning and benefit of touches of color is to spend time looking for them in the environments you inhabit. Stand in the doorway of a room and scan the room for things that pop out at you. Notice their color. Color will usually pop in relation to another color. For example, green will pop against a black background. Red will pop against a blue or green background. Yellow will pop against a red background.

It is the touches of color that give works of art their visual interest and energy. Treat your working environment as a work of art by adding touches of color, and you'll find you are happier and more productive working there.

Like anything else, too much of a good thing ends up not being a good thing. Because touches of color can be so powerful, too many of them can be distracting and make a space feel chaotic. Use touches of color strategically rather than generously. When there are too many of them the effect of any one touch loses its effect in the overall sea of color.

Treat your working environment as a work of art by adding touches of color, and you'll find you are happier and more productive working there.

Chapter Four

Lighting

"What would Debbie do?" My client, Julia, says she asks herself that when she gets stuck. Then she knows what to do. She flips the light switch. "Debbie says when you can't think, add more light. Add more energy to get your brain working!"

It's always a thrill to be given proof that I've made a difference for a client. I stood across the room with a smile on my face, marveling that Julia had internalized what I'd said, and used it to move herself forward.

For years I have instinctively begun many a session in some pretty grim environments by flinging open curtains and turning on every light in the room. I do anything I can to increase the positive energy in the space to a point where I can think.

The brain finds it very difficult to work effectively in spaces loaded with clutter, dust and grime. The negative energy of those spaces just shuts the brain down. Long ago I learned that adding light, natural or electric light, lifts the energies in spaces. Then the brain can kick in and get the body moving. Granted, it brings to light some pretty challenging environments, but that is a necessary step to tackling any organizing project.

Our brains are stimulated by light. A well lit space is necessary for optimal performance and productivity. Check it out. Attempt to do a complex task in a dim environment. Pay attention to how you feel as you begin the task. You will likely feel somewhat irritated; as though you need to jump start your brain. The brain does not perform well in low light.

I came to this realization as I worked in a client's closet, trying to clear months of clutter from the floor. I kept experiencing the urge to run away. I recognized that I was shutting down. Instead of giving in to that urge, I stopped and asked myself what was bugging me.

The answer was that I couldn't think clearly because the lights weren't working properly. I was working by light streaming in from the bathroom on one side and the bedroom on the other side. The lack of positive energy in the closet made just being in that space intolerable. Trying to organize a mound of clothes, which required more brain power, was impossible. Once I realized that I needed more light, I moved the bulk of the clothing from the floor of the closet into the well-lighted bedroom and sorted it there.

Light is essential for optimal performance. A combination of natural light and artificial light works best.

Natural Lighting

Have you ever worked in a space with no windows? Your natural habitat is the out of doors, so you literally crave the light of the sun. When you are deprived of it for any length of time your energy tends to diminish, your mood dips, and you begin to seek natural light.

If you worked in a space without windows, you would probably find yourself longing for your lunch break or the end of the day when you would be released from your cave. Even if you work in a well lit room with full spectrum lighting, you'll still crave natural lighting. Your nervous system thrives on it.

When I begin a session with a client, the first thing I do is make sure there is adequate natural lighting, if it is available. I uncover the windows to let in light that lifts the energy of the space to a point where both my brain and that of my client work optimally.

Artificial Lighting

Ideally, natural lighting provides the foundation of light in a space and artificial lighting augments it. It usually takes both natural and artificial lighting to make spaces comfortable and effective as work places.

Guidelines for Using Artificial Lighting

- ***Avoid fluorescent lighting*.** Though economical and effective in providing bright light, fluorescent lighting stresses the nervous system because it is not full spectrum light and it usually makes low level noises, pops and buzzing sounds. Spending time under fluorescent lighting leaves people feeling exhausted and irritable.
- ***Avoid halogen lighting*.** Halogen bulbs provide a harsh light that can irritate the nervous system.
- ***Use incandescent lighting*.** Incandescent lighting from lamps, overhead lights and track lighting is recommended because it feels like natural lighting. Lamps, in particular, provide pools of light that mimic the light you might find outdoors in a forest, thus making you feel more comfortable.
- ***In an office with fluorescent lighting*, *keep the overhead lights off and provide light with at least three lamps.*** For optimal lighting, make sure that the lamps can use 100 watt bulbs. Have at least one pole lamp that throws light on the ceiling.

When I make these recommendations I am often asked why I don't recommend green and economical lighting solutions. I am a firm believer that personal safety and health must to be a top priority of any interior solution, followed by green and economic considerations. Incandescent lighting provides adequate light without unduly stressing the nervous system.

Lighting that has a negative effect on the nervous system in turn affects the immune system because everything is connected. If the immune system is damaged, a person is vulnerable to many physical problems whose impact could be far worse than the financial and environmental cost of using incandescent lighting.

Chapter Five

Condition of Space

The condition of a space has a profound effect on performance. Spaces that are in good condition have a predominance of positive energy and minimal sources of negative energy. That positive energy directly affects your energy.

Spaces that are in poor condition have a predominance of negative energy. The energy of poorly maintained things dominates that space, distracting your attention and lowering your energy level.

To illustrate, let's compare two offices. The first office was painted two years ago and has clean, unblemished wall surfaces. The hardwood floors are clean and polished. Furnishings are of different ages, but have been well maintained and are clean and fully functional.

The second office has trim that is peeling. Painted wall surfaces have many marks on them. The carpet is dirty and worn. The furnishings are of different ages and several of them have many scars and water marks on them.

Which office would you want to work in? Where would you find it easier to work in a focused, deliberate way? Granted, I am describing opposite ends of a spectrum to make a point. But, my guess is that you felt at least a slight dip in energy as you imagined the second scenario. Just thinking about these spaces affects your energy. Your energy drops when you think about the poorly maintained space and lifts when you think about the well maintained space.

Can you see that the actual condition of spaces matters? It affects the quality of interactions with others. It affects how clearly you think and make decisions. And, it affects whether you can work or not.

What is the condition of your work space? Start by looking at the condition of the overall space and work your way to the condition of the individual objects.

Signs of a Space In Good Condition

- Clean
- Unblemished painted walls and other surfaces
- Flooring and carpeting in good shape
- Functional, well maintained furnishings

When you walk into a space, you get an immediate feel for the condition of the space. It's as if your brain has a barometer that automatically reads the energy of the space based on the condition of the walls, floors and furnishings. Has the space been well maintained?

Signs of a Space Whose Condition Needs Improvement

- Dirt
- Peeling paint
- Worn rugs and floors
- Dirty floors
- Broken or damaged furniture

Scissors

As you might expect, improving the condition of the walls and floors in a space will have a greater impact on performance than improving the condition of individual items. Big changes create big results. But, don't underestimate the effect of smaller items that are not in good condition.

Because everything is connected, the negative energy of one wobbly table can profoundly affect the energy of a space. You will also find that once the condition of the walls and floors has been improved, the negative energy of furnishings that are in poor condition will be much more obvious. Their negative energy will pop out at you. Don't be surprised if you feel the urge to fix everything whose energy is negative.

Chapter Six

Individual Items

Now, let's look at the individual items in a space. One of the keys to creating a high performance environment is to be deliberate in choosing the furnishings, decorative items and other objects that fill the space. Unfortunately many spaces fill up without thought or conscious awareness that each thing in a space has an energy that can enhance or detract from the intended function of the space.

Scissors

Getting conscious of what you have in your space is an important first step to getting a handle on creating a high performance space. That means taking a look at everything in the space and evaluating it for its usefulness and significance.

Types of Items Found in High Performance Environments

- Things that serve the function of the space
- Things that have positive energy because of their appearance, condition, their associations and their usefulness
- Things that fit comfortably into the space
- Things that bring the outdoors inside

Aspects of Items

There are three major aspects of items to consider when evaluating the things in your space:

- Energy
- Quantity
- Arrangement

Note: Energy is the primary and more complex aspect of items, therefore many pages of this section are devoted to explaining it. A discussion of quantity and arrangement follow the discussion of energy.

Energy

The energy of an item can be read in three different ways:

- Positive or negative
- Condition – What is the condition of each individual item?
- Association – Does the item have an association? If so, is it positive or negative? How strong are the feelings that the association elicits?

Positive or Negative Energy

Characteristics of things with positive energy:

- Loved or used
- Good association
- Good condition

Characteristics of things with negative energy:

- Not loved or used
- Negative association
- Poor condition

Items that are loved or used have positive energy, energy that will serve you as you work to accomplish your goals. When an item is not loved, it has a negative energy. When an item is not used, its energy dies. Dead energy is negative energy. Negative energy blocks opportunity and forward progress.

High performance environments have a majority of things that are loved or used and few things that have a negative or dead energy.

Love It

Loving things gives them energy. Terah Collins in *The Western Guide to Feng Shui* says, "Love it or use it." I modify that statement and tell my clients to "Love It, Use It or Lose It™!"

People tend to love items because they:

- Were a gift from a special person
- Hold a special memory
- Hold a special association
- Are aesthetically pleasing
- Engender a special feeling

People tend not to love items because they:

- Remind them of an unpleasant time or experience
- Were given to them by someone they dislike or who dislikes them

I can tell when an item has "love it" energy by my client's tone of voice when they talk about it. Their voice lifts and has a soft, warm and enthusiastic tone. It often reminds me of the purr of a cat.

An example of a "love it" item is a beautiful paperweight that was a gift from a special client. In this case the feelings of love come from both the beauty of the item and the positive association with the client.

When an item doesn't have "love it" energy, the client's voice is more matter-of-fact or even flat. It's as if the light inside them goes out. Very often their eyes and their head will be downcast. They'll sometimes groan as if expressing the burden of the decision about what to do with the item.

An example of an item that is not loved is a drab painting with no particular significance. You dislike the style of painting and its drabness is depressing to you.

Some items have mixed energies that make determining whether or not they have "love it" energy difficult. For example, you've kept a vase because you love the friend who gave it to you. However, you don't really like the vase. The association is positive, but its energy is negative.

At this point it's important to assess your feelings about the object. If your spirits lift when you look at it because it always reminds you of your cherished friend, then the positive energy of the association dominates. If the first thought you have is, "How could she pick something so ugly?" then negative energy dominates.

Use It

Using things gives them energy. The energy of an item that is not used goes dead over time, unless it has "love it" energy. Homes and offices are filled with things that have dead energies. One of the best ways to energize a space and thus energize the person working in the space is to clear out items that aren't being loved or used, leaving the space filled with only those things that are alive with energy.

How often should you use something to keep its energy alive? A good rule of thumb to keep the energy of an object alive is to use it at least once a year.

Condition of Items

As described above in the section about condition, it is optimal that every item in your space be in good condition. Items that are in good condition have a positive energy. Items that are not in good condition have a negative energy.

Good condition does not mean perfect condition. You know something is in good condition when it functions as it was meant to function, without any hassles, and its appearance in no way disturbs you.

Consider, for example, a sturdy filing cabinet. The drawers open and close easily; it has a few scrapes on its exterior that you hardly notice. That filing cabinet is in good condition. A perfect looking desk with drawers that stick is not in good condition. A desk that functions well, but has a bleached out, scarred top, is not in good condition.

Things that are not in good condition have negative energy. If they can be restored to good condition, great! If they can't be restored to good condition, their negative energy will have a negative effect on your energy and your performance.

Association

As you become more conscious of your space and its effect on your energy and performance, you can check to see if each item has a positive or negative association. That association affects the energy of the object. For example, a diploma that makes you feel proud of your years of hard work has a positive association and a positive energy. A table that was built by your ex-husband, with whom you had and still have a painful relationship, may have a negative association and negative energy.

The most telling way to determine the strength of an association of an object is to listen to the first thoughts that come to mind or the first words that pop out of your mouth when you look at and evaluate the importance of a particular item. "I got that from my father the day I graduated from college. I'll never forget how annoyed he was that day because we were stuck in traffic. . ."

Strong associations just pop out. For example, Martha's first words when I asked her about a dresser in her bedroom were, "My ex-husband used that." She didn't say, "That's a dresser I bought at IKEA" which was also true. I was already aware of the intensity of pain associated with that relationship, so those few words spoke volumes.

The association keeps the energy of the item alive, positive or negative. If you are checking the energy of things by yourself, watch your thoughts. If there is a strong association, the thoughts will automatically pop into your head. Then you can decide whether that memory/association really serves you or whether it keeps you stuck in a painful place.

Some items hold several associations and it's important to determine which association has the strongest energy. For example, my ex-husband, Dave, made me a coffee table out of a slab of yellow birch. He made it when we were living in Vermont for a year, working with my father who had a sheep farm and a small maple syrup operation. Ed McPhee, a local resident who helped my father in many ways and did logging in the area, gave Dave a big slab of yellow birch and suggested that he make it into a table. Dave did just that and presented it to me as a Christmas gift.

The following summer Dave and I moved back to Utah when my father decided to stop raising sheep and making maple syrup to return to the field of medicine. That table rode back to Utah in the back of our Volkswagen Rabbit, all 85 pounds of it!

When Dave and I were divorcing and dividing up household possessions, he thought he should get the table because he made it. In a moment of strength during a very painful time I told him, "You'll get that table over my dead body! You made that table for me. It's the only thing you ever made for me." I won that argument and the table is still a focal point in my family room.

When I consider the associations that the yellow birch table holds, there are several strong associations. First, there is the association with Vermont and our year long adventure in that beautiful state. Then there is the association with Ed McPhee, a generous, helpful, down-to-earth man who made our time in Vermont much more interesting and sometimes more tolerable. There is also the association with Dave's hard work to create the table. It holds positive energy about his effort to make me a very special gift. There is the association of both Dave and me loading that heavy table into the back of our Rabbit, sharing our good feelings about the table. It also holds the negative energy of the memory of him wanting to take it back. Then there is the energy of the memory of me standing up to a husband who bullied me psychologically.

With all those associations, especially the association with my ex-husband, you may be wondering why I still want to have the table. When I look at that table, the association that speaks to me the loudest is the memory of an incredible year in one of the most beautiful places I have ever lived. And, the uniqueness and beauty of the table are what I notice every day. The fact that Dave made it for me, and that he wanted it back when we divorced are details that hold much less energy. I am only aware of those associations when I make an effort to recall the story of the table. So, the table stays. It is one of my priceless treasures!

High Energy Items

When putting things in your space, take the time to read their energy, consider their condition, and determine if they have a positive or negative association. Consciously choose high energy items because their energy will have a positive effect on your energy. They make a space feel more comfortable. When a space feels comfortable, everything that happens in that space is positively affected by that energy.

Following is a list of high energy items to add to your home or office:

- Objects of nature
- Light sources
- Sound makers – chimes, bells, fountains
- Flags
- Animals
- Mirrors
- Brightly colored objects

Objects of Nature

I attended an annual conference of the National Association of Professional Organizers in Reno, Nevada. As I moved through the hotel lobby I found myself repelled by the glitz of the decor. When I ventured into the casino I felt disoriented by the cave-like space with the mirrored ceiling, busy carpet pattern, and noise of the machines. I was told that casinos are deliberately designed to encourage people to gamble. They are intentionally designed to be disorienting. What a strange place to have the annual conference of a group of left-brained, highly organized people!

As I looked around I was struck by the lack of connection between people. All around were people sitting alone at machines or focused on games at tables. It all seemed incredibly sad to me. I couldn't wait to get out of the casino each time I had to walk through that space.

What a contrast it was to go upstairs to the conference rooms! Gone was the noise and glitz. It seemed like any other conference center – pretty lifeless. Up there we spent time in windowless rooms and ballrooms divided by partitions. Although those rooms were clean and functional, they lacked natural light, color and positive energy. When I emerged from those caves for a break it was such a relief to look out large picture windows at the mountains in the distance. I stood at those windows and drank in the view. The contrast between the man-made environment and nature had never been so evident to me.

People can create all kinds of environments. Without an inkling of consciousness about how we are affected by those environments, we can spend enormous amounts of time in spaces that are not life-affirming. For most of us it's not a casino, but our home or office. One quick way to improve the energy of those spaces is to bring in elements of nature. Add a print of a beautiful landscape. Add plants and water features like fountains and aquariums.

I was in a windowless bathroom recently that came alive with shell prints, real shells and a silk plant. Nature feeds our souls in ways that man-made, lifeless environments cannot.

A human being's natural habitat is the out of doors. Therefore, when you bring the outdoors inside, in the form of plants, rocks, shells and water; you feel more comfortable. When you feel more comfortable, you perform better.

To bring the outdoors inside add:

- Live or silk plants
- Art with scenes of nature
- Water fountains
- Rocks
- Shells
- Driftwood
- Fabrics with plant patterns
- Blue and green colors
- Fresh flowers

Light Sources

Light sources were discussed in the previous section. They are high energy objects, but they only enhance a space when there is a comfortable balance between light and dark in the space and they burn brightly without flickering, buzzing and glare. A space with too many bright lights is uncomfortable. So, too, is a space lit with bulbs of low wattage. Insufficient light makes it harder to think and get things done. Therefore, it is important to remember that a light source, which does add energy to a space, can be used in a way that it is actually perceived as an irritant, as negative energy.

Sound Makers

Anything that makes a pleasant sound has positive energy and can be used in the creation of a high energy environment. Common examples are bells, chimes and water fountains. Use sound makers with care because what might be a pleasant sound to you may not be a pleasant sound to other people. Your perception of the energy of a sound maker will depend on the quality and the frequency of the sound.

A gurgling fountain is a steady sound. If the pump is inaudible and the water flow is gentle and soft, it becomes a lovely background sound reminiscent of an outdoor stream. If, however, the pump is noisy, its sound can be very irritating. If the water flow is rushing, it can be distracting at best or could stimulate the urge to relieve yourself at its worst.

Flags

Flags? You may be wondering why I would address flags when discussing interior spaces. Flags can be great sources of both color and movement, and they are affordable. Both color and movement can be high energy sources in an environment. And, flags can be used inside. Flags can be hung on a curtain rod and mounted as a wall hanging.

The benefit of using a flag is that its movement is subtle and gentle. It is made of fabric which brings an interesting texture to a space. Because flags don’t require a great investment of money, they can be changed more often than other art pieces. You can change them when you change and want to reflect that change in your space.

Animals

Cats, dogs, fish and birds can be high energy sources because they move around in the space, keeping the natural energies of the space moving. As with other high energy sources, which can swing to low energy sources under specific conditions, animals are only high energy sources when well cared for, healthy and, in the case of dogs, when well trained.

When I visit one of my regular clients I enjoy greeting her cockatiel, Sonny. He's very personable. The area around his cage is always neat and clean because his cage has a special skirt that catches seeds that otherwise would litter the floor. It's always a positive experience to see Sonny.

Another client's daughter begged for a bird, but when she got it, she wasn't able to keep its cage and the surrounding area clean. Because the bird lived in her bedroom away from people, it constantly squawked for attention. Though it was a beautiful bird, its behavior and the mess it created were definite sources of negative energy.

Mirrors

Mirrors always add energy to spaces. They bring in light and can make a small space feel larger. They resemble pools of water and can make spaces that seem hot feel cooler. Smooth, flat mirrors are preferable to beveled mirrors or mirrors broken into smaller panes by cross members which can throw light and energy in many directions. Large mirrors should be placed at a level that reflects the whole head of anyone looking into them.

Brightly Colored Objects

Color is nurturing. Brightly colored objects bring in those essential touches of color that feed you with positive energy. Include things with colors that pop out at you when you look into your space, colors you love, colors that lift your spirits.

When colors fade, it's time to repaint or let the object go. Faded colors make objects look worn out and then are a source of negative energy.

Low Energy Items

As you become more and more conscious of the energy of things in your environment, you are likely to find yourself wanting to eliminate low energy things because they actually pull on your energy, depleting it over time.

Examples of low energy things include:

- Broken things
- Irritating problematic things
- Faded or worn things
- Dirty things
- Things that aren't loved or used.

The process of eliminating low energy things is described in the Paper section of this book.

Quantity of Items

What is the ratio of things to the size of your space? Is the quantity of things appropriate for the size of the space, less than appropriate for the size of the space, or more than is comfortable for the size of the space?

Have you ever walked into a room and had the urge to turn and bolt from the space? One possible reason for that type of discomfort is that the quantity of things in the space overwhelms it. You are most comfortable when there is a pleasant balance between the number of items in a space and the amount of open space. When there is little open space, most of the energy of the space has been consumed by the things in the space. You may find it difficult to breathe and to think there. When you can't breathe or think, it's normal to feel the urge to run.

Less is more. It is easier to think clearly and make good decisions in spaces that are uncluttered, those that have what's needed to serve the function of the space and nothing more. Unfortunately, consumerism has led to people accumulating too many things for their homes and offices. Busyness keeps people from making the time to sort and release unwanted and unnecessary items. Because each thing has an energy that you are aware of at some level, their energy can distract you from your work. It may feel like you are trying to work in a crowded subway.

Creating a high performance environment requires paring down items to just the quantity that feels comfortable in the space. There is no magic formula for achieving an optimal level of comfort. However, feeling irritated or distracted when working in your space is a sign that you may need to reduce the number of objects there.

I work from a home office that is filled not only with functional furnishings and equipment, but also artwork and decorative items that are important to me. Because the speed of incoming items always exceeds the speed of outgoing items, every so often I stop the work I'm doing and clear out my office in an attempt to make it a quieter place to work. Over time it's as if my office goes from having just a gentle murmur of a quiet conversation to feeling like a noisy classroom. When the noise of all the things in my office gets to me, I clear. Regular clearing keeps me functioning!

The Arrangement of Items

How things are arranged affects their energy and in turn affects your energy and your perception of those things. Following are common arrangements found in most spaces. Notice the polarities of positive and negative in each of the following pairs of arrangements.

Homeless or Distinct Home

Ideally every item in a space has a distinct "home." A home is an assigned location for that item. An ideal home for an item is one that is easily accessed based on frequency of use and/or is aesthetically pleasing. When items have a distinct home, you can find them.

Homeless items have either not been assigned a distinct home or have been removed from their home and have not been returned to it. Homeless items often become the bud of clutter. If left for long that bud will attract more homeless items and a full blown clutter puddle will grow.

Floating or Anchored

Things that float are not located in their designated homes. They are out of place. We are most comfortable when all items are anchored to their designated locations.

A most annoying arrangement is one where pieces of furniture are not positioned up against a solid wall. When big pieces are floating, the whole room feels chaotic and it's very difficult to work effectively in the space.

You work best when you feel grounded. When things in a space are anchored in a specific home, the space feels grounded and comfortable. When a space is grounded, you feel grounded.

Cluttered or Organized

Barbara Hemphill, author of *Taming The Paper Tiger at Home* and *Taming The Paper Tiger at Work* defines clutter as "postponed decisions." Clutter is an accumulation of things that are out of place. Its energy is chaotic and overwhelming.

When items are organized, they are strategically clumped by type and function, placed in a specific location and often labeled. Organized items have a positive energy. Best of all, they can be found when needed!

Scattered or at Right Angles

Picture a desk covered with papers with no particular order. Then picture a clear desk with a single neat pile of paper on one side of the desk. You probably felt at least a stir of anxiety as you contemplated the desk with papers scattered all over it. When papers are scattered at many different angles, they have a negative chaotic energy, the kind that can make you want to do anything but work with them.

Papers gathered together in piles and placed at right angles to a desk have a much calmer energy even if the papers aren't organized. When I encounter papers scattered over a surface I instinctually gather them into a pile on one side of the surface, quieting their energy and calming myself with that action. Then I am better able to face the task of addressing the paper.

You work best when you feel grounded.

Chapter Seven

Position

Where you position yourself in a space affects how well you perform. You may have noticed that people tend to avoid putting desks in front of open doors. They intuitively know that they are not comfortable working in front of a door. Most people also avoid placing their bed in front of a door. Why is that?

Your nervous system is programmed to assure your safety and survival. The nervous system is most relaxed when you have a solid wall behind you and a full view of the door. That way you are protected from behind and you can see any potential threats. You are in the power position, ready for anything.

Many people assert that they are completely safe in their home or office. So why does your position matter? You may rationally know that you are safe, but your nervous system is still operating to protect you. It only relaxes when you are in a position of complete safety. When you are in that position, all your energy can go to your work instead of having a portion of your energy devoted to self-protection.

Position made a huge difference for a client named Dave. When I worked with Dave, he was struggling in every aspect of his life. He was in the middle of a nasty divorce. His wife made it difficult for him to see his children. He changed jobs and struggled both in his new position and financially. In desperation he asked me to help him with his apartment.

The first thing I noticed was that his sofa was missing its legs. I believe objects in our space anchor the energies that affect our lives. In Dave's life he felt cut off at the knees by his wife and his circumstances. No matter what he did, he could not move forward. The sofa looked like it was cut off at the knees, just like Dave. It was holding the energy of disempowerment in place.

When we got to Dave's bedroom, neither the desk nor the bed was positioned with a full view of the door. When seated at the desk, his back was to the door. There was no solid wall behind him and no view of the door when he worked at the desk. The bed did have a solid wall behind it, but it was positioned without a full view of the door.

The sofa, bed and desk were the pieces of furniture Dave used most. All three had significant positioning problems that affected his ability to be fully empowered.

To help Dave move from disempowerment to empowerment, I recommended that he replace the legs of the sofa and move the bed to a wall that allowed him a full view of the door. Because it's not a good idea to have anything associated with work in the bedroom, I also recommended that he move the desk into the second bedroom, placing it with a solid wall behind it and a full view of the door.

When I saw Dave about six months after our consultation, I hardly recognized him. He told me that he had followed my recommendations and that his whole life had turned around. He made peace with his ex-wife about their children. He went back to his old job where he was very happy and successful. And, he was happily involved in a new relationship.

Scissors

To assure peak comfort and performance, make sure your most-used pieces of furniture, typically the bed, desk and sofa, are placed with a solid wall behind them and a full view of the door. That positioning affects how you view the world and how you feel about yourself. And, how you feel about yourself has a direct effect on performance!

Chapter Eight

Views

Mary had spent years creating a comfortable office, one where she could work well and that she could maintain with a little help from me. Surprisingly, Mary told me that she was avoiding her office since beginning major renovations on her house. I suspected that the reason for her avoidance of her office was that the room had been changed as a result of the renovation.

As I entered the door of Mary's office from a peaceful screened porch, I saw a clothing box deposited in front of her desk. A number of other boxes and baskets were also strewn in front of the desk. Her familiar and comforting books had been removed from two bookshelves so that breakables could be safely stored there. The chaos of the entry area of that room made me want to back out the door. When I stood on the side of her desk that faced the door, what I saw was also anything but harmonious and peaceful. I was looking at the back side of the same chaos that I'd seen from the door. No wonder Mary was avoiding her office! It's pretty normal to avoid sights that overwhelm us.

Mary and I had work to do at her desk, but I knew we needed to transform the new chaos before either of us could tackle the desk work. We began by sorting the things by the door, many of which could be moved into her current living area. I covered the clothing box with an attractive throw and put a plant on top of it.

We cleared out that area until all that was left as a greeting was a small table with a welcoming green plant. That done, we both sighed with relief. The room had been restored to an energy level that was welcoming and positive. It wasn't what it had been before the disruption of the renovation, but we succeeded in transforming the most negative aspects of the disruption into an appealing arrangement. The chaos that pushed Mary from the room was gone.

Stand at the door of your office or any room in your house. What is the first thought that comes to mind as you gaze at what greets you? Are you thinking positive thoughts? Notice how you feel. Do you feel peaceful, empowered and proud or distracted, exhausted and overwhelmed? Does the room invite you in to make progress on the tasks you must do? Or, does it push you away and shut you down with its confusion and disarray?

What is the first thing you see when you enter your office or a room in your home? That's the greeting. What kind of greeting is it? Is it welcoming or off-putting? Normally the area or objects with the strongest energies will pull your eyes to it. Strong negative energy will beat out strong positive energy every time. Remove those sources of negative energy to make sure you have a positive greeting in each room.

Views inform you. They set the tone for what can happen in the space. They can invite or repel you. Changing views for the better will improve performance every time.

Consider All Views

All views have some effect on performance. The view from the door you use to enter your house and the view into each room are the primary views affecting your house. The view from the front door is also very important even if you routinely enter through the garage or a side door. Secondary views that affect performance are views out windows.

The primary views that affect offices are the view into the office and the views from the desk out of the room. Secondary views are the views out windows. For example, consider the effect of looking out at a well maintained landscape. The positive energy of the view out the window becomes part of the overall energy of the room. Positive energy equates with positive performance.

On the other hand, a view of an overgrown lot with dead shrubbery and broken equipment adds negative energy to the room and can have a negative effect on performance. An elementary school teacher who heard me speak about the importance of having natural light in the classroom came up to me after my speech and told me that she keeps the blinds in her room closed all the time because there are bars on the outside of the windows.

That view was so disturbing to her that she chose to block it altogether. Blocking a view that you cannot change is one way to reduce negative energy. The tradeoff for the teacher was that blocking the view also blocked natural light, a source of positive energy. The teacher reported that she was having a very difficult class that year. I suggested that she open the blinds of two window sections at the far end of the room to see if the addition of natural light would help improve the attitudes of the children. Another option was to explore whether the bars could be removed.

When a view is problematic, fix it if you can or block it with a screen of some sort. In a home sheer curtains work well because they make the view blurry but still let in light. At the very least, place furniture so people occupying the space aren't positioned to look out on a poor view.

Changing views for the better

improves performance every time.

Part III

Paper

"To change skins, evolve into new cycles, I feel one has to learn to discard. If one changes internally, one should not continue to live with the same objects. They reflect one's mind and psyche of yesterday. I throw away what has not dynamic, living use."

Anaïs Nin

Wouldn't it be nice if you had a clean slate to work with to create a high energy, high performance environment? Unless you are in the process of moving, you will first have to address the accumulation of objects and papers in your space before you can consciously create a high performance space.

Paper

Those of you who are by nature organized and disciplined to maintain a clean and orderly space have far less work to do than those whose spaces are less organized. Starting with a space that is well maintained and free of things that no longer serve you is a big advantage. However, I find that once organized people learn about the relative energies of everything in their space, even the most fastidious can find numerous things to clear before they set up a new arrangement.

This section describes the complex process of clutter clearing. In my experience, clutter clearing is the most significant barrier to achieving a space that invites and supports optimal performance. Once a space is clear of items that no longer serve you, addressing problems with the condition of the space and arranging the space for comfort and peak performance is much less daunting.

You may find yourself seized by the urge to clear clutter as you read this section. If you are, **stop reading** and begin clearing. This book will still be waiting for you, but the energy of the urge to clear may not be. Take advantage of it when it hits! Then watch for the energy of your space to shift from negative to positive. And, notice how your ability to think and function effectively increase.

Chapter Nine

Clutter Clearing

One of the best and easiest ways to start the challenging, sometimes overwhelming, process of creating a high performance environment is to clear clutter. Often you may have the intention to create a high performance environment, but you can't quite make yourself get started. Perhaps you're baffled about where to start. Or, you may feel overwhelmed when you look around a room and realize how many decisions must be made in order to make the changes you really want.

Clearing clutter removes items with dead or negative energy that can block clear thinking about your goal and how to reach it. Clearing clutter helps you get clear mentally.

Why Clear?

We survive by taking in food, air and water and excreting wastes on a daily basis. We stay healthy as long as we take in good food, air and water and regularly excrete wastes. If we take in things that are not good for us, like unhealthy foods, polluted air and toxic substances like excessive alcohol and drugs, over time we become sick. If our organs that eliminate wastes and toxic substances, the liver and kidneys in particular, become diseased and stop working properly, toxins back up in our system and we become sick.

I learned the principle of food and water in, wastes out when I was a child. My father was a nephrologist helping people whose kidneys were diseased and no longer excreted wastes well enough to keep them healthy. I remember looking at those people hooked up to dialysis machines that circulated their blood and removed the toxins. Their pallor was sallow and had a greenish tinge.

To this day I say a prayer for anyone who looks like that. I know they are sick with a chronic illness. There is nothing that can be done, save get a kidney transplant, to make them better. They often depend on a machine to live. Even then they have severe restrictions on what they can eat and drink. What a horrible existence! It was clear to me as a child that if you can't excrete wastes properly, you could die. And, certainly many of those people died much sooner than they would have if they had been able to efficiently eliminate wastes.

Our houses, like our bodies, are living entities. Things quite naturally flow into our houses. You don't even have to work at getting things to come in. For one week, pay attention to the quantities of things flowing into your home. In one day, at the very least there will be mail. Add to that, the flow of personal items for every family member. And, if you are into shopping, watch out! Day after day of that influx results in an increasing accumulation of items. Without being conscious of it, and without conscious effort to manage the flow of those items, your house begins filling up.

Healthy homes are those in which there is a regular flow of things both in and out. There is a regular release of wastes in the form of garbage and recycling. But, that's definitely not enough to keep a house healthy. That is just the tip of the iceberg. To keep the energy of a house looking and feeling good, there must also be a regular outflow of things that are no longer used or loved.

You might be saying, "Duh! I know that! Of course stuff must go out." But, are you deliberately doing it? Many of us have gotten so busy with the pressing demands of work, raising a family, dealing with ailing parents and keeping up with regular maintenance tasks, that we are just not conscious of the press of our belongings. We keep stuffing things in closets, drawers, attics, garages and basements to ease the pressure, but we never really relieve it! We think we don't have time to address the quantities of stuff that are building up.

Guess what? The enormity of the task increases exponentially the longer you put off doing it. And, you pay a hefty price! The more things you have in your house that no longer serve you, the sicker your house becomes. Sick houses affect the people who live in them! For example, clients of mine who have the most stuff have a higher incidence of chronic illnesses than clients with fewer possessions.

Like the human body, to maintain a healthy house you **must** excrete wastes on a regular basis. Wastes in the home or office include garbage and recycling plus anything that no longer serves you, anything that you no longer love or use. Many things you save because "I might need it someday," fall into this category, the odd part, the bits of string, the ancient appliance that you never use. You save them, but fail to organize them for easy access and they take on a dead, negative energy.

Your Energy – The Key to Success

Everything is connected. So, you can have the best of intentions and schedule the time to organize only to find that all your chi (energy) has already been consumed by life's many demands. If you don't have energy to use for the physical and mental tasks of clutter clearing, you won't get much done. In fact, feeling tired is an all too familiar excuse to do something less taxing.

You may be thinking, "How taxing can it be to 'clean up'?" Even if the task is not particularly physically demanding, the mental challenge of figuring out what to do, how to do it and making thousands of decisions can wear anyone to a nub, myself included.

In order to successfully clear clutter, you will need physical energy and a clear head. Fatigue is a very common excuse to avoid or quit clearing clutter. At best, fatigue can slow the process to glacial speed. If you find yourself feeling weary (often a steady state for the adrenalin junkies many of us have become), you can lift your own energy to a higher level.

I recently found myself standing in my kitchen feeling exhausted. I had helped friends move the day before and had depleted my energy reserve. I had work to do to create order and peacefulness in my home—important tasks like laundry, cleaning, changing bed linens.

As tired as I was, I felt overwhelmed by the many tasks before me. None of them were difficult to do, but with low energy I felt more like taking a nap than tackling my maintenance tasks. I counseled myself to do what I would urge a client to do in this type of situation. I went inside myself searching for a way to generate some energy. Almost instantly a thought popped into my head, "Turn on the music." I knew music would shift my energy. Within minutes of listening to some energetic classical music I snapped out of my exhaustion, got moving, and eventually completed all my chores.

Music is just one way to lift your energy. You can accomplish the same thing by adding light by either turning on extra lights or opening curtains and blinds. Spaces that aren't adequately lit can keep the energy of the space low and, therefore, keep your energy low. It's a simple thing to add more light. Bring in extra lamps if you need to.

Exercise also lifts your energy. Especially if you tend to be sedentary, a quick walk around the block or a private dance to your favorite music in the living room can be enough to wake up your energy.

Eating something can help if you choose your food carefully. It's important to avoid simple carbohydrates like starches and sugary snacks. Those foods can give you an initial burst of energy, but that burst is quickly followed by a drop in energy. Fresh vegetables and fruits can be refreshing with fewer side effects. Be sure to eat some protein because protein is brain food. It helps your brain function efficiently to think clearly and make good decisions.

Drinking water or decaf herb tea is preferable to drinking coffee or caffeinated soft drinks. Caffeine can make you feel alert, but if you drink too much caffeine it stresses your system and actually can exacerbate fatigue.

Another way to lift your energy is to get rid of things you don't use or love, things that are **easy** to give away or throw away. Remember, everything holds energy. As you clear things from your space, the energy that they were holding is released and is then available to you. For this reason I urge clients and audiences to whom I speak to remove items that have been identified for purging immediately. The sooner the items are released from the space, the sooner you will feel an increase in energy. The day after a major purging, I am always flying high with extra energy.

I love watching clients' energy increase as together we make decisions about what to keep and what to pitch. They often go from having very low energy and very few ideas about what to do with their belongings to becoming excited about their progress and full of ideas about possible solutions to their organizing challenges.

Finally, if you can't get your energy up after trying the above suggestions; invite a trusted friend, family member or professional organizer to help you. Your energy responds to the other person's energy. The interaction itself is usually enough to get you moving. With the help of a respectful person, a boring task can be transformed into a pleasant social event with a great outcome. Just remember your goal and use the energy generated by the interaction to get the clearing done.

Chapter Ten

Never Start with Paper

Why not start with paper? It's often the biggest problem in spaces where work is to be done.

Take out a piece of paper. Look at it carefully. Imagine that you have a stack of papers just like that one. You have to make a decision about each piece of paper. Should you keep it? Should you toss it? Imagine how long it would take you to see progress dealing with hundreds (maybe thousands) of sheets of paper? A very long time! Do you think you could maintain your momentum through your project if you start with paper? No!

Paper

Think back to your previous organizing attempts when you did start with paper. How much progress did you make? Clients regularly report failed organizing attempts when they start with paper. Why? Most people become overwhelmed and quit.

Exception: You may start with paper if it is the only thing you need to clear.

If you start with paper, you will quit. You'll run away! You'll go shopping, watch TV, eat a cake or decide the lawn just has to be mowed right now. Paper will shut you down.

I learned that starting with paper is a **big mistake** the hard way. A client hired me to help her get organized and wanted to start with paper. At our first appointment she had at least four boxes full of paper to process. I was a relatively inexperienced professional organizer at the time and followed her lead.

We both began sorting and Mindy made decisions about what to keep and what to toss. I quickly learned that Mindy had extreme difficulty getting rid of any paper.

At about an hour into the process Mindy looked up and assessed our progress. We had worked our way through one quarter of a box. Have I mentioned that doing paper is not only boring, but also enormously slow? At $40 an hour, a huge sum for a receptionist, this project was looking like a very expensive venture.

With a panicked look on her face Mindy expressed her concern about how long it was taking to get the job done. Naively I said, "I can make it go faster."

I can sort very quickly, so I suggested that I do all the sorting and Mindy decide what to keep and what to throw away. That sounded like a reasonable plan to both of us. We worked along for another hour and a half until Mindy got up and began taking deep breaths in apparent distress.

When I asked her how she was doing she told me she was having an asthma attack. I thought, "Oh, great! I've put my client into a life threatening situation." Madly wracking my brain for some way to help, I asked if she had something she could take to stop the asthma attack. She grabbed an inhaler and took a puff. Then she gagged, covered her mouth and ran to the bathroom where she proceeded to throw up.

You see, unbeknownst to me, **every** piece of paper had significance to Mindy. Letting go of any of it was very difficult. To let go of so much paper in such a short period of time was traumatic for her, truly terrifying. And, it was a terror that made no sense to her and that she could not explain to me. Somehow she was comforted by the paper. It held her history. It somehow grounded her. It also drove her crazy and held her back from functioning in her life in the way she wanted. But, at that point she was not capable of just casually throwing it away.

I learned some valuable lessons from that one troubling session. But, the most important lesson was, **Never Start With Paper!**

Believe it or not, despite that traumatic start to our relationship, Mindy and I worked together over a period of two years. At that point, she was ready to take some big steps in her life and she moved away. But, we never started with paper again. We made it a point to organize other things first and finished our sessions with a little paper sorting.

The only way to effectively deal with paper is to back into it. In other words, don't tackle it head on. Have a blast evaluating, sorting and purging everything else in your space first. Then when the room is feeling great and all that's left to do is sort and clear paper, you'll find it easier to handle the paper.

Notice I didn't say it would be **easy** to do paper. It will never be easy. It requires more mental focus and carries the added burden of the possibility of negative consequences if you make an error in judgment about what to keep and what to toss. It's exhausting to process paper, particularly in large quantities.

Start with Big Stuff First

Big stuff includes furniture, audio-visual equipment, books, clothing, framed art, empty boxes, anything of significant size. When tackling any organizing project like clutter clearing, it is imperative that you see visible progress immediately. Seeing progress is the only way to stay motivated to continue doing work that is challenging and overwhelming.

Over the years I've observed that my clients instinctively first reach for things that are most difficult to address, probably because those things have the most distracting and demanding negative energy. Usually they reach for paper which just screams with negative energy. And, the idea of getting the worst over with first is a good one. But, because clearing clutter and getting organized is challenging both mentally and physically, the top priority should be to see visible results even if it means dealing with things that are easy to sort and pitch.

Feeling Overwhelmed? Do What's Easiest!

I am sometimes asked if I ever get overwhelmed. My answer is always a resounding, "Yes, of course!" And then I share the story of my first visit to Beth.

When Beth called to schedule an appointment, she shared that she was at risk of being evicted because of the condition of her apartment. Management considered her apartment a fire hazard. Given that information, I knew I was in for a challenge.

I had received calls like that before, from people who have extensive disorder, but most canceled before the appointment date. If I were to guess, I would say they probably canceled because the thoughts of having anyone see how they lived was just more than they could handle. People often say, "Oh, I could never have you come help me. I'd be so embarrassed."

To Beth's credit, she didn't cancel. I am sure the threat of eviction was an effective motivator. She greeted me warmly and welcomed me into her living room. I always carefully monitor my facial expressions and comments when I first walk into a client's home or office. I know clients watch me carefully to assess my reaction to their space. In this case I had to work very hard to keep my expression neutral.

The room was completely packed with an immense volume of items of every sort, so packed that I had to step carefully so I wouldn't be walking on her belongings. I later learned that there was furniture in that room, but I wasn't able to see it for the clutter that day. I knew work with Beth would be a challenge like none I had thus far encountered. To say I was overwhelmed would be an understatement. I had difficulty just catching my breath.

What does this story have to do with energy? If you recall everything has energy. In this case I was confronted not only by the chaos of an extremely disorganized space, but also with an incredible volume of disorganized items. The quantity of negative energy was paralyzing. It really stopped me in my tracks.

My first thought was, "How can I possibly make a difference here?" The sheer enormity of the challenge rendered me speechless for a few moments. In moments like that I have trained myself to breathe and pray. Taking deep breaths calms me. Praying grounds me and helps me get back to my own center to be able to access what I know.

As I prayed, I scanned the space looking for a clue about where to start. I knew to look for big stuff to move so we could experience a positive shift of energy and become more motivated to tackle the big job before us. Unfortunately, the biggest stuff, the furniture, was well buried. Then I noticed that there were some large empty boxes scattered throughout the rooms. Beth's habit was to open boxes of things she'd purchased through the mail, and just leave the box wherever it had been opened.

With Beth's permission and help I began flattening the boxes and moving them to the front door. It was an easy task to do because Beth had no need for the boxes or any sentimental attachments to them. And, they were light and relatively easy to remove. By removing the boxes we immediately were able to open up areas in several rooms, release some negative energy, and create hope that creating order over time was possible.

So, when you find yourself feeling overwhelmed, look for the biggest, easiest thing that you can move. Often that is all it takes to break through that overwhelmed feeling and get moving.

Apply the Love It, Use It or Lose It™ Method

Terah Kathryn Collins introduced me to the idea that we thrive when we live with what we love or use. In her book, *The Western Guide to Feng Shui*, she recommends that you "love it or use it" if you plan to keep a particular item. I modified that statement to Love It, Use It or Lose It™. In other words, when evaluating an item during clutter clearing, ask yourself, "Do I love this?" If you don't love the item, ask yourself, "Do I use it?" If again the answer is no, then consider losing it. Throw it away. Give it away. Clear it out of your space.

The love it and use it aspects of this method were discussed in the Scissors section, particularly in describing things to have in a high performance environment. High performance spaces have a preponderance of things that are loved and/or used. So, what things should you lose?

Lose It

Items to lose are those that you don't love or use. People tend not to love things because:

- The things remind them of an unpleasant time or experience.
- The things were given to them by someone they dislike or who dislikes them.
- They feel a sense of obligation to keep the item when the item does not function as it should.
- They have outgrown them. Memorabilia such as records, clothes, sports equipment no longer hold their interest.

As mentioned previously, clients' voices tell the truth about items that they no longer love. When they don't love an item, their voices have little inflection.

An example of an item that is not loved might be a gift that you dislike, given by a cherished friend. You've kept the item because you love the friend. The association is positive, but the energy of the item is negative. If the negative energy of the item is stronger than the positive energy of the association, get rid of the item.

Items that aren't used at least once a year often have a dead energy. It's easiest to feel the effects of dead energy once you have cleared things that you no longer love or use from a space. In the absence of dead things you'll find yourself energized and ready to take action. Although you may not be conscious of things whose energies have gone dead from disuse, those dead energies do affect your ability to think clearly.

For example, I've worked with clients who are occupying an office that had been occupied by another employee who left files, books and other papers behind. I helped them clear out the old, dead energies of the former employee. Unfortunately, the norm in the workplace seems to be that new employees hit the ground running, ignoring the files and papers left behind by a former employee. The thought usually is, "Oh, I may need that information. Someday I'll go through it."

What I experienced when I began new jobs and what I observe in clients is that new jobs are all-consuming. Most people figure things out on their own and rarely touch the old files, much less use them as a valuable resource.

It's great fun for me to help clients look at the old files and release them. Without exception, every client who has evaluated the value of those old files has ended up purging almost every one of them. By the time they got to those files, with my help, they were ready to let them go. There was no question of whether they might need them some day. They knew what they needed. By then the only question was how fast could we get those dead things out of their space.

As we released the old files that had become a burden even though they were untouched, I watched clients' energies shift. Initially they might carefully examine each file, but by the end of the process they were tossing things in the trash with enthusiasm. Their energy increased as the dead items were released. They genuinely seemed relieved to finally be free of the burden.

Unbeknownst to my clients, those papers and files also carried the weight of predecessor chi (energy). They held the energy of the previous occupant. It was as though the ghost of the previous occupant was still present. The office wasn't totally theirs until the items belonging to the former employee were processed, purged and/or integrated with the new employee's files, books and papers.

Things to Be Purged

Broken Things

Broken things clearly are sources of negative energy. You usually feel some negative feeling when looking at or dealing with something broken. You may feel irritated, annoyed, frustrated, burdened with one more task to be done, angry, even tired.

Broken things hold the energy of brokenness and can attract being broke (financially) or being physically broken (health problems). Remember energy attracts more of the same. Broken things also require work on your part. First you have to decide if a broken item is worth fixing. If so, you have to figure out how to fix it. You might need to find someone to fix it. You might need to take it to a repair shop, and on and on. Do you get the picture? The best thing to do with broken things is to either fix them quickly if they are worth fixing, or to pitch them in the trash.

Static Things

Static is defined as having no motion. Static things don't move. Things that don't move are likely to have dead energy. The exception, of course, is something that you love. Many things that are loved don't move because their energy comes from aesthetic qualities or positive associations. However, if an item is not something you love and it's not being used at least once a year, it's likely to be static.

You can find static things in every drawer, cabinet or closet in your home. The largest collections of static things are usually found in the large, out of the way storage places like the attic, basement, or garage.

The common categories of static things that are often found in large quantities are: paper, books, memorabilia (the kind you find in boxes in the attic), clothing, and photos. Of these static things, be sure to start your clearing with a category that is easy for you to do. For example, if you really love books, start with clothing. **Don't start with paper.** As we already discussed, paper is the hardest to do and it takes much longer to make progress with paper than with larger items like books or clothing.

Anything with a Negative Association

When you look at an item and it reminds you of a person or an event that makes you feel mad or sad, it has a negative association. For example, my husband once gave me a basket of silk flowers on a day when we had had a big fight. He appeared at my office mid-morning with a pretty basket of silk sunflowers, apologizing for his behavior. I accepted the basket and his apology and put the basket in my office.

Some time later after I'd learned how to read the energy of objects, I was evaluating everything in my space by asking myself, "Do I love it? Do I use it? What's the association?" And, guess what the association of that basket of flowers was? Fight! When I looked at those pretty sunflowers I thought, "I wouldn't have these flowers if we hadn't had a fight!" They held fight energy. Because I knew that energies tend to attract more of the same, I got rid of the flowers. I certainly didn't want to attract more fights with my husband!

As you move through your space, check out the associations of everything. Pay particular attention to the first thoughts that pop into your head when looking at an object. Those thoughts often hold the association. Are those thoughts positive or negative?

You might find that some objects hold more than one association. In the case of my basket of flowers, one association was that Bob used those flowers as a means to apologize for his hurtful behavior. That was nice. But the other, much stronger association was the fight association. Because the negative association was stronger, I chose to give away the flowers.

By getting rid of anything with a negative association, you clear negative energies and create a space in which to thrive and attract more good things to you.

Make Things Go Away Quickly

The most important thing to remember about the Lose It step in the Love It, Use It, or Lose It™ method is that the full benefits of clearing occur **after** you've removed the items that you "lose" from your space. Many people clear a space but fail to empty the garbage. Or, they clear a space and leave the items to be donated in bags in their home, garage, attic or car trunk. If those items are still anywhere in your space, you won't receive the full benefit of the clearing.

Make "lose it" items leave as quickly and easily as possible. Things you have in your space affect what happens in your life. An energy block, like clutter, can block good things from coming to you. Clearing the block makes it possible for more good things to come to you. Drawing out the process of removing the items from the space will only postpone making space for good things. Meanwhile, all that accumulated negative energy screams at you!

Trust that items you plan to give away will end up in exactly the right new home without your having to make it so. It's not important that those items be given to exactly the right person. The more individual deliveries you make of your purged things, the more you are postponing making progress and gaining positive energy. Choose a charity. Drop your things off, and let go.

Unless you are a "get it done" kind of person who can put together a yard sale in a matter of days, don't hold onto things for a yard sale. Saving things for a yard sale is like building a concrete wall around yourself, blocking the flow of new good things to you. It's rare that yard sales happen quickly because doing one requires planning and advertising in addition to accumulating sufficient items to make your effort worthwhile. I sometimes find prospective yard sale items hanging around in garages for years after they were identified as such. Release those items and watch your life start moving again!

Get Started

By now you understand the Love It, Use It or Lose It™ method and you're psyched about creating a high performance space. You know you should start with big things. Now what?

Start with the biggest item in the room. Check its energy. Ask yourself, "Do I love this?" If you have no special emotional attachment to the item, ask yourself, "Do I use this?" If the answer is no or not in the last year, consider losing it.

As soon as you decide to eliminate an item, remove it from the space. Preferably place it just outside the door. It's not a good idea to pause in the evaluation process to take the item much further than outside the door because you risk getting sidetracked doing something else.

Removing the item from the room releases the energy that the item was holding. It is then available for you to use as you continue to make decisions about what to keep and what to release. As you make decisions and move things out of the room, your energy increases and making decisions becomes easier. Your brain begins to generate creative new ideas about what you can do in your space.

When you find that removing things from the room is getting difficult because so many things are outside the room, reward yourself by stopping the sorting process temporarily and taking those items to their respective locations. Do not stop to reorganize the new location even if you cannot easily put the item away. Just leave it in the area and make a mental note that the area needs attention at a later date.

It sounds so simple, doesn't it? If that's the case, why do people avoid clearing clutter? How do their spaces become nightmares right before their eyes? Because it's simple, but not easy. Clutter clearing involves making so many decisions. You not only need to decide what to keep and what to pitch, but also where to start and what to do with all your things as you work. It can be a great logistical challenge with the potential for distraction everywhere.

When I work with clients, part of my job is to keep them from running away. Even though I am in charge of the process and make it easier for them, they are still affected by the way the space feels and by the enormity of the decision-making process.

Too Many Conversations!!!

Are there so many things screaming for your attention that it is impossible to zero in on what you love or use? My approach to dealing with a space that's screaming with a million conversations is first to silence the conversations. The things that "talk" the loudest are little, tiny items (coins, jewelry, keys, toy parts, scraps of paper) and paper.

Paper makes the most noise, especially if it's spread all over the place. I recommend gathering all the loose paper together in a box or bag(s) and setting it aside. **Do not** stop and read any of it. You just need to harness its negative energy and put it aside to be handled later. Your space should be noticeably quieter once you have stopped the chatter of all the loose paper. Then look for loose little items and put them in a basket or bag. Don't bother to put them away immediately. Your goal is to lift the energy in your space by silencing the many nagging conversations coming from items that are just lying around.

Once you've corralled the paper and little stuff, then you are ready to address the space as a whole. Begin by determining the function of the space. A bedroom, for example, usually has three functions: rest, changing clothes and intimacy. First look at the furnishings and other objects to determine if there is anything that doesn't fit the function of the room. This is also a good time to consider whether there is anything that you do not love or use. Objects that are loved or used are more likely to have good energy. If you don't love or use it, it is a candidate for release.

Once you have sorted items by whether they stay or go, you can move on to sorting them by type. All CDs go together. All books go together, etc. When items have been clumped by type you can get an accurate picture of the quantity of individual items that you own. When you realize you have twelve pairs of black shoes or three copies of the same book, it's easy to let go of some of them.

You need to know **what** you have and **how much** you have before you can find permanent homes for everything. Each object needs a permanent home that makes sense and is easily accessed;

then both the objects and their arrangement have positive energy. When you get this far, you will feel energized because you have eliminated all the sources of negative energy. When you get to the point where all you have in your space are those things that have positive energy, and they're organized where they can be found to be used or enjoyed, you will feel empowered.

The Fallacy of Time

Clearing clutter takes time. Excavating a neglected space can take an incredible amount of time. I remember spending two hours sorting the contents of three drawers for a client. Areas that melt down over time and become disorganized masses of stuff truly take more time to confront and resolve than most people have day-to-day and week-to-week. On the other hand, putting items back where they belong on a daily basis usually takes just a minute or two. Yes, you have to do it over and over again, day in and day out. But, doing that ensures that you don't end up with a nightmare of your own making.

We all have avoided doing an unpleasant task because we thought it would take forever to do and we just couldn't face it.

When we finally made ourselves tackle the chore, we found that it took much less time than we expected.

I remember helping Elsa clear out a bathroom that she had neglected for months. It was loaded with a huge tumble of dirty clothes, cosmetics, toiletries and cleaning products on the floor and on every flat surface. It was also filthy. Dust and soap scum combined to form grime everywhere that was truly off-putting. It was very difficult to face. It looked like a job that would take days to do.

Focusing on the big items first, the clothing and towels, we saw immediate progress. The task Elsa had avoided dealing with for a month was put in order in 45 minutes.

That kind of progress would not have been possible had Elsa been working alone. It did require a professional who knew where to start and how to make things happen quickly. But, this story clearly demonstrates that the timeline in your head, the one you form when you look at the mess before you and imagine the work that must be done, may not be accurate. If you use an effective process for clearing clutter, it can happen more quickly than you expect.

Visit a Clutter Free Friend for Motivation

If you want to get motivated to clear clutter in your home or office, go visit a friend who is a minimalist – one of those people who keeps things so simple that their space feels stark to you. I speak from experience! My husband, Bob, and I went to help our dear friend, Frank, with a few chores in his garden. It was my first visit since he had moved into his condo, so he showed me around. He was putting his new home together with great thought and care. There was no clutter, except in the guest room which housed all the unfinished projects. There were very few decorative items, very few pictures on the wall, very few rugs. Of course, he wasn't finished creating his space, but given what I had seen so far, I knew it would still be sparsely furnished and decorated when he was finished. That's what he likes.

When I got home to our cozy little ranch house, I couldn't help but compare the feeling of his home to our home. I wouldn't be comfortable living in a home like Frank's, but seeing his home, and more importantly, feeling his home; I realized that I did want more simplicity in my home. I wanted fewer things out in the open, fewer things talking to me energetically.

So, the next day, before I got caught up in the busyness of my office, I rearranged my supplement drawer so I could move a collection of supplements off the kitchen counter into the drawer. At least one surface was more peaceful. I also kept looking for items that I could either give away or pack away for later use. The influence of Frank's space lasted for months as I kept paring down extraneous items from our home, gradually creating a more peaceful environment.

The next time you find yourself in a calm, clutter-free space, instead of whipping out the bat to mentally club yourself for your clutter, use that energy to go home and whip a cluttered spot into shape! That way you too will benefit from the positive energy of a clutter-free space.

Trust that items you plan to give away will end up in exactly the right new home without your having to make it so.

Chapter Eleven

Getting Going

You promised yourself that today was the day you would tackle the clutter in your home. You wake up thrilled at the prospect, right? Wrong! How many people want to spend their precious spare time sorting through the debris of their lives? So, how do you get yourself to do it? Promises aren't enough. Good intentions aren't enough.

I am one of those strange people who actually get a thrill out of clearing out a closet or drawer. Why is that, you might be asking yourself. I think it's because I am very conscious of the shift in energies that happens when I do it. A space that felt irritating, burdensome, and inconvenient is transformed to one that feels fresh and new and functional. I love making spaces feel better. When I clear a space I create a new clarity and eliminate one thing in my home that is bugging me. Clutter and chaos in my space bug me. When I take a few moments and create a new order, I create more peace for myself.

Granted, the overall level of order in my home is pretty high, given that my DNA seems to have an organizer gene and I am pretty conscientious. The quantities of clutter I deal with are pretty small compared to what I see in clients' homes. It's easy for me to start a clearing project compared to many other people because I am less affected by the overwhelm factor.

So, what do you do if you have lots of clutter and you feel overwhelmed? First, remember that doing something is better than doing nothing. What you do may not produce stunning results quickly, but doing any clearing shifts energies in a positive direction.

Second, set a small goal for yourself. For example, plan to work for ten minutes. Set a timer and go to work. When the timer goes off, stop. Most of us can work for ten minutes. During that time do whatever is easiest to create some new order. And, I don't mean turn on the television! Throwing away trash is usually easy. Clearing off a table might be easy. Finding a bag full of things to give away might be easy.

Third, congratulate yourself on your success. That sounds silly, doesn't it? Some of you are thinking, "So, I did ten minutes of clearing in a house that needs ten weeks of clearing. What's the big deal?" The big deal is that you made a plan to clear and kept it. You got started. Every bit of work helps. And, if you don't stop and feel the good feelings that come from the accomplishment of the work, how are you going to motivate yourself to continue? It's a head game. Play it!

Fourth, schedule your next clearing session, preferably sooner rather than later. Repeat the process. All progress makes a difference as long as you aren't creating more chaos between sessions than the amount you cleared.

So, You're Stuck. . .

I'm sure you can think of a time when you approached a particular cleaning or organizing challenge and found yourself immediately feeling overwhelmed and quickly backed away from it.

Perhaps it was a pile of papers, a loaded closet or a room so disorganized that it made you want to run out of the house screaming.

Actually, the size of the mess is one factor that affects your ability to move forward and create order. The bigger the challenge, the more overwhelming it is likely to be. Another factor that applies to any size organizing challenge is the condition of the mess. Is it a clean or dirty mess? The energy of a clean mess is higher than that of a dirty mess. Is it made up of a mix of big and small items or just small items? A mix of small items has a frenetic, confusing kind of energy that rarely fails to make people want to run away.

Susan, a regular client and a busy mom with Attention Deficit Disorder, asked me to help her with a small pile of paper that was probably less than three inches deep. The pile contained loose papers, catalogs and notebook paper that had been cut into small pieces. She took one look at it and turned to me and said "Debbie, please help me with this. I can't do it."

Now, I'm talking about a vibrant, intelligent, college-educated woman who is doing an incredible job raising five children. What shut her down? On examination, I realized it was the small pieces of paper. Though they had no writing on them (which would have complicated dealing with them), they put off an irritating negative energy. That energy blocked her from accessing the rest of the pile. Once I identified the culprit and threw the paper away, Susan was able to face the pile and make the decisions necessary to clear the rest of it.

If you find yourself avoiding clutter clearing, take a moment to see if you can identify what is shutting you down. Is it a boring mess – like paper? Is it a full of overwhelming little things? Is it a filthy job? Are you clueless about what to do with the stuff? Are you really exhausted and unable to think clearly? Identifying what shuts you down is the first step to moving forward.

Big Picture Shutdown

One way you may be shutting yourself down is by looking at the whole space and everything that must be done to return it to a functional, comfortable place to live and work. If you are one of those big picture people who can only see the forest and not the individual trees, you actually blow yourself out of the water when you look at the whole challenge in front of you. It's just too much to take in. Taking on the whole picture at once shuts down even the most intelligent, determined person.

Long ago I learned what I affectionately call the Monkey Grass Technique. I actually discovered this technique when I was cutting a large bank of monkey grass in my yard.

The whole task was enormous; something to be avoided at all costs. Being very visually oriented and highly motivated to enjoy the look of the front of my house, I set out to tackle that bank with knife in hand.

I diligently sawed off the old leaves. Quite unconsciously I kept my head down and moved steadily along the bank from right to left. Only very occasionally would I glance up to measure my progress, and only for a second. I just kept my head down and my mind focused on the progress I was making instead of overwhelming myself with thoughts of how much more there was left to do. Because I refused to allow myself to look at the whole task to be done for more than a few seconds and I refused to allow myself to think that I couldn't get it done, I was able to make steady progress and finish the job.

The lesson of the monkey grass is to keep your head down, focus on the task at hand, and avoid looking at the big picture except for small snapshots. When you do look at those snapshots, congratulate yourself on progress made and silence thoughts about how much more there is to do. Celebrate the small victories of the progress you make, and before you know it you'll be done!

Emotional Blocks

In some cases being stuck has emotional components. Therefore, when I work with clients who claim to be stuck, I look very carefully at the content of the items.

For example, are we clearing the remains of the client's previous job? If so, was the job a positive or negative experience? Was leaving the job a choice or was the person asked to leave? When people leave jobs it's very common to turn all their energy to finding a new job or to adjusting to a new job. They postpone going through the things they brought home from the old job. Those items hold the energy of the old job. Because the person has moved beyond that job, the energy of those items naturally diminishes. Over time it becomes harder and harder to find the energy to go through those things, clear the clutter and integrate useful items into the client's living space. In addition, whether a job was positive or negative, leaving it involves losses, usually on many levels.

Most of us instinctively avoid feelings associated with losses. One way to do that is to shove the box into a corner to be dealt with later. If the leaving was particularly painful, the urge to avoid will be stronger. And, the consequences of holding onto the stuff will be greater. Why? Because the old job stuff holds the energy of that experience.

When you peek into the box, memories assault you. What energy do those items hold in place when a leaving was negative? They might hold, "you are incompetent" energy or "you just weren't appreciated" energy or "you're a failure" energy. Those negative energies can keep you very stuck. You probably are not conscious that they have so much power over your ability to act.

Whether or not you are conscious of it, avoidance of clutter clearing often happens because the items that make up the clutter to be cleared are related to a serious loss. The most common examples are death, divorce, trauma and job loss.

Items hold the energy of the person (a spouse, mother, father, sibling, dear friend, or child) or experience (job loss, death, divorce, or trauma) associated with them. If those things are moved, as they must be when you are sorting to clear clutter, the energy of the person or the experience often is accessed. Memories may come to the surface. Those memories are likely to elicit feelings – feelings that perhaps have been avoided for a variety of reasons and for a long time.

Jesse, a client, had an easy chair sitting in the middle of her home office. Because it looked out of place, I asked her several questions so I could help her determine if it should stay in the space or be moved elsewhere. When I asked her how she used it, she told me clients would sit there occasionally, but then admitted that she really was ready to part with it.

When we attempted to remove that chair from the room we weren't able get it out of the door. Jesse insisted that it had come in the room without taking the door off. After several unsuccessful tries we decided that our only option was to remove the door. We had no luck there either. The bolts that held the door in place were stuck. "One more try," I said. To our astonishment, the chair sailed through the door with remarkable ease.

Looking back, it seemed as though the chair had been resisting leaving the room. And, for no apparent reason, it gave in and chose to leave. We were both amazed. When we got to the bottom of the stairs with the chair, Jesse remarked, "That was my ex-husband's chair."

The story of the chair was that her husband had sat in it night after night when he came home from work. It was loaded with his energy. Though Jesse had chosen to end the marriage, unconsciously she had kept her ex-husband close by until she was ready to move on. I warned her that she might feel some deep sadness that the chair had been holding in place. She later told me she was glad that I had warned her because that night she accessed the deep pain of loss of her marriage and the loss of the possibility of reconciliation because her ex-husband had died. Jesse donated the chair to a charity and was then free to fully grieve the loss of her marriage.

Releasing that chair was an important step for Jesse. Releasing it facilitated a release of feelings that were cluttering her ability to think clearly and move forward with her own life and business.

In another situation I was working with Marcy to clear papers that had accumulated in her office. Once again she was stuck! What I found right in the middle of the stack were papers associated with her mother, now deceased. I'm sure Marcy was not conscious of the source of her shutdown. But, paper associated with someone significant who died holds the energy of the loss. Why would she want to face that?

When you've made a commitment to clear clutter and you find yourself hitting a wall, stop and ask yourself, "What is this about? Is there something here that I'm having difficulty facing because of loss?" Then stop, be still and listen to what comes up for you. It may just be that you're tired or don't know what to do, but be open to considering a deeper reason. Is some sort of emotional pain halting you in your tracks?

If you realize you are being stopped because there is pain associated with the items you are touching, stop and allow yourself to acknowledge it. Feel it. Notice that the pain is still alive. Leaving the things untouched will only anchor the pain to that spot. You may choose to walk away and leave it for now. Perhaps just noticing it and feeling it is all you can do right now.

When you are ready, make a plan for how you will release the pain. One option is to decide that you'll tackle three items per day. Keeping the volume low will limit your exposure and allow you face the pain at a measured pace.

Perhaps the emotional issues are too big to face alone. You may need the help of a non-judgmental person who can just be with you while you face the feelings that come up. I often invite clients to hold onto those things that are too emotionally loaded until our next meeting. Then we go through them together. They have my support and encouragement to face their losses and associated pain and, if it feels right, they can tell me the stories associated with the pain.

So often just putting words to what happened can release the power of the pain. When they're ready I help them figure out how to transform those things that have so much power over them into something else. Some things will go to the trash or be given away. Others will be selected to be transformed into something positive like a scrapbook.

Freedom is the reward for recognizing an emotional roadblock, facing it and respectfully dismantling it. It's as though you are taking back part of yourself that was being held hostage, being shut down without your conscious knowledge. After you acknowledge the grief and release the pain you will probably feel lighter, have more energy, and be ready for new challenges and adventures.

Rearranging Things Can Get You Unstuck

One Monday, Sylvia wanted me to tackle organizing her home office. What a way to start the week! She said it felt like it was closing in on her. I really dreaded going up to her home office to work. It was packed with many boxes of unprocessed paper, boxes of audio cassettes, exercise equipment and other miscellaneous items plus two desks, three filing cabinets, a small refrigerator and a book shelf. I'd worked there before, creating a basic order by clumping like things together. However, it had been some time since I'd worked there and I knew the order had probably melted down to a general disorder. I also knew that what was really needed was for Sylvia to work with me to really make a difference in the space. She preferred for me to do it on my own and on this particular day she wouldn't be arriving home until an hour after I arrived. So, up I went to see what I could do.

I worked hard for about an hour, recreating recognizable clumps of audio cassettes, VCR tapes, CDs, paper, computer reference materials, cords, miscellaneous items and paper. When Sylvia finally arrived, she let me know that she needed to make room for a new fax machine and some reference books. The only location for those items was on the desk without the computer. My challenge was that the desk was piled about three feet high with papers associated with Sylvia's roles as a professional speaker and exercise instructor.

I love challenges like that! I was determined to move those papers somewhere else. Why? Not only did I need the space that they occupied, but I knew that just moving those papers would set the energy of that office in motion. A new order would help Sylvia in some way. Moving that paper and creating a new space for things that Sylvia would use shifted the stagnant energy in the room. Getting rid of papers that had been there for over a year released positive energy into the space.

I found a place to neatly place all the paper from the desk. I labeled reference binders and placed them on the desk with the new fax machine and an adding machine that hadn't been used because there had been no place to plug it in. Not only did that corner of the room feel better, but the whole room felt better! Sylvia now finds it easier to work in her office. And, I no longer dread working there.

A new order can create optimism and movement. If you feel stuck during a particular project and have difficulty purging things, at least rearrange what you have and feel the energy shift and move you!

Remove Blocks

In some cases a specific block disrupts the energy flow in your space. Once that block is removed, you are able to figure out what to do with a space. I remember first becoming conscious of the existence of specific blocks when I was helping Darcy, a young waitress, organize her bedroom.

As I looked at the cluster of organizing products and quantities of clutter in her bedroom I noticed that the containers seemed to form a wall across the space between the doorway and the bed. Talking with Darcy I learned that she'd recently broken up with a boyfriend and was once again living alone. She admitted to feeling afraid alone in her apartment at night. Out of fear she had unconsciously built a wall around herself for protection. Unfortunately, while the wall did provide a sense of safety, it also blocked energy from flowing into her room. She needed that energy to motivate and energize her to create a new order and rebuild her confidence.

Another example of the power of identifying and removing an energy block occurred when I was working with a couple who recently established a home-based business selling pools. As I contemplated the large family room that served as an office/ showroom, I was at a loss for how to arrange the room for maximum benefit and function. I felt brain dead. The room was furnished with an enormous big screen TV at one end, a cluster of hand-me-down living room furniture in the middle, and a desk, filing cabinet and other office equipment at the other end.

Mark, who was the driving force behind the business, used the desk. I knew that his desk would need to be placed in the power position, with his back to a solid wall and a full view of the door, if the business was going to take off. As it was, his desk faced away from the front door of the room toward sliding glass doors on the far side of the room. I started with that challenge.

After considering various options, I realized that there was no way his desk could be placed in the power position. There was only one solid wall in the room, and his desk was currently placed in front of it.

I didn't consciously know it at the time, but the desk was an energy block. It kept us from seeing the best way to arrange the space. It didn't work well where was. And as long as it stayed there everyone, including me, was stuck – unable to organize the space. Once I determined that the desk really didn't belong in that room at all, I went searching for a better place to locate it. Fortunately, there was a "junk room" nearby that with some clearing and rehabilitation was easily converted to a functional office.

When the desk, office equipment and big screen TV were moved into the new office, we were able to quickly determine the best function for the family room and what should remain in the space. It would serve a dual purpose as the location for Mark's assistant's work space and a showroom for pools. Our decision was confirmed by the ease with which Mark's assistant created a work area for himself. Within minutes he was set up and ready to work. We then placed a demo spa in one corner with plants behind it. I put the finishing touches on the family room by quickly clearing clutter and setting up a work station and storage area.

Removing Mark's desk from the family room altogether was the key to being able to use that room in a way that worked well for Mark and his assistant individually and for the company as a whole. It went from cluttered and jumbled to an attractive showroom once the block, Mark's desk, was removed.

Types of Blocks

When I go into spaces where clients complain that they are stuck, I routinely search for energy blocks. I look for an item that, if moved, will allow energy to flow again and bring life-giving inspiration.

Blocks come in many forms. A particularly problematic pile of paper can be a block. A piece of furniture with a negative association can be a block. As in Mark's case, the block can be that an item just doesn't work where it's located, but removing the item completely hasn't been considered. Blocks can be powerful because of their physical or their emotional/psychological size. When you find yourself stuck, ask yourself, "What's the block here? What is keeping me from moving forward?" You will know you've found the block when you move it and suddenly find yourself on a roll, making significant progress.

Sometimes the block is not one particular item, but the result of too many items in the space. I was invited to the home of

Hannah, a Mary Kay consultant and busy parent, to help her clear and organize her home office. When I walked into the small office in her third bedroom and looked around the space, I started feeling disoriented and spacey.

At first I felt alarmed that I was unable to access my brain. After all, I was being paid to figure out how to help. I said a quick prayer for help as I looked around the space, hoping I'd be inspired. Then I noticed that there was more furniture in the room than was comfortable for that size room. The furniture was holding onto so much of the natural energies in the space that there was not enough energy left to allow me to think clearly. With Hannah's help we identified a piece of furniture that was least useful in that space and moved it to the hall. When I returned to the room, my brain was back, activated by the energy released by removing that piece of furniture.

If you find your thinking is blocked, fuzzy or spacey, remove something sizable from the room. It doesn't have to make a permanent exit, but pulling it out of the space will shift the energy of the space and allow you to move forward. Once you've made progress, cleared out unnecessary items and created a new order, the item can be returned if it works well in the space.

Freedom is the reward for recognizing

an emotional roadblock, facing it

and respectfully dismantling it.

Chapter Twelve

Getting Help

Getting help is something most people avoid. After all, fierce independence is part of our culture. Some people believe that if they know what to do and are physically capable of doing it, they should do it.

On the other hand, I have watched countless people stay stuck or work far below their potential because they refused to get help. I, too, struggled with the, "I can do it myself" mentality, which by the way, reminds me of the words of a two-year-old in the middle of an independence tantrum. Then I realized that some very important things were not going to get done at all unless I got help.

When I needed to do a press release to announce my new organizing business back in 1998, I kept avoiding the task. I am a capable writer, but writing about myself and my business was an overwhelming task for me. I finally broke down and hired a marketing consultant who drafted the press release and got it published. Mission accomplished!

Not only did the job get done, but the consultant suggested I create a booklet to offer as an incentive to anyone who contacted me about my services. Her idea resulted in the booklet, "Simply Organized: The Art of Conquering Clutter." By accepting help I not only got my press release done, but I got the idea and the motivation to create my first product for sale. The money I've made from selling that booklet has more than paid for the cost of the consultant. That makes me wonder if I can afford not to ask for help from qualified others!

Now when I find myself avoiding important tasks that affect my well-being or the well-being of my company, I hire someone to get me unstuck. I am a firm believer that people should work within their areas of strength and hire people to do those things that they:

- Hate doing
- Don't know how to do and don't care to learn how to do
- Are not capable of doing
- Are not good at doing.

Being stuck in the process of clearing clutter equates with being stuck in your life. Until you can see your way clear of the physical and emotional blocks in your environment, it will be difficult to move forward in your life.

So, if despite your best of intentions and your best efforts, you just cannot get a clearing project done; it's time to get help. That could mean calling in a friend or family member to help you get started, or hiring a professional to do the job with you.

Body Double

An economical way to get help is to find a body double. According to Judith Kolberg, author of *Conquering Chronic Disorganization*, a body double is a person who functions as a human anchor, someone who helps you focus and ignore distractions.

Having functioned as a body double hundreds of times with clients, it seems almost magical that clients who cannot face a task alone will tackle it with me present. My being there makes a difference.

Years ago, when my husband was working in a paper intensive job, he would occasionally reach crisis points and would ask me to come into his office to help him. At first, I thought he wanted me to organize his office for him. But when I arrived he invited me to take a seat in a chair in the corner of the room. He then went to work. He didn't need me to do the work; he just needed me to be there with him. Somehow my being there calmed his anxieties so he could go to work.

A good candidate for a body double is someone who is willing to be with you while you work. It must be someone who understands that you are in charge and they are just there to hold the space to make it easier for you to work. They must be non-judgmental and supportive, willing to do small, supportive tasks that you ask them to do. And, they must be committed to helping you get things done, not be distracting. Parents, spouses and siblings often do not make the best body doubles because there can be power struggles and judgmental attitudes in those relationships.

I am a body double for a good friend who struggles with Attention Deficit Disorder. I stopped by for a visit one day on the spur of the moment. After she served me tea she zipped around her house, straightening up, washing dishes, doing all those tasks that she couldn't make herself do when she was by herself. I watched with amusement because I knew she was making the most of an unexpected body double. She understood the concept of the body double and took advantage of it whenever it was available.

Facing Paper

Who loves organizing paper? No one. Let's face it; paper is the number one organizing challenge for everyone! Even very organized people struggle to keep up with the barrage of paper coming their way on a daily basis. Hopes that the computer would reduce the amount of paper were quickly dashed as people began printing out emails and other documents "just in case" their data was lost.

Paper

Not only is paper universally a major clutter clearing problem, but disorganized paper is at the top of the list of things that have negative energy.

Why is the energy of disorganized paper so bad? Let's consider a pile of paper containing a mixture of items. When you look at the pile, it tells you nothing specific about itself except, "there's work to be done" or "there may be something in here that you are forgetting" or even worse, "you are so incompetent because you don't keep up with this mess." Now, one pile alone can be quite intimidating, especially if you know there are important items in it and you can't seem to make yourself deal with it. Many people have paper spread throughout their houses, complicating the task of keeping up with it. The paper acts as a source of negative energy wherever it has landed. The further afield it is spread, the harder it is to address. Its negative energy has the power to shut off activity. It's as if you spread a wet blanket over everything.

What do you do when you experience paper paralysis, when you are stuck in your efforts to clear clutter and you know paper is part of the problem? Cathy's office comes to mind when I think about paper paralysis. Cathy is a creative person, a writer and a busy mother of two children. Much of her house is well organized and attractive. She called me to help her get a handle on paper. She had never been successful organizing paper in her home and she was ready to enlist professional help to set up a paper management system and learn how to keep her paper organized.

Cathy's office was in a light and airy sunroom that was quite large. At one end were her desk, computer and filing cabinet. A love seat and a partially dismantled file cabinet were at the other end. Paper was strewn from one end of the space to the other. Some of it was in piles, some in bins, some in files, and some was loose – just lying on the floor. It looked like someone had loaded a cannon with paper and had shot it into the room.

As I am in the habit of doing, I asked Cathy if the paper was already organized in some way. Believe it or not, some really disorganized spaces can have some sense of order. If that had been the case, destroying the order could have traumatized her and set us back in our organizing efforts. In this case, however, she laughed and said, "Oh no." That was the answer I was hoping for.

With Cathy's approval I gathered all the paper into bins and boxes, separating out office supplies and miscellaneous objects that were mixed with the paper.

How would you have tackled this project? Most people would have picked a pile and grabbed the first piece of paper off the top, perhaps working their way through the pile. How long do you think it would take to see progress using this approach? Hours, days…a lifetime! More likely, after considering several pieces of paper, you would have a compelling urge to do anything to avoid the enormous challenge of making decisions about every single piece of paper. Doing laundry would have more appeal than sorting paper page by page!

Experience has taught me that the way to handle paper is to make sure you reduce its negative energy and see immediate progress by reducing the size of the area that it covers. When we finished boxing up all the paper, creating an initial order, both of us gave a sigh of relief. Whenever you stack paper in neat piles you eliminate quantities of negative energy and replace it with the positive energy of a tidy open space.

When Cathy and I arranged the furniture to best support her office activities, we created a positive foundation for handling the paper challenge. Usually, I would have first organized the office supplies we had unearthed, again doing the big stuff (and easier stuff) first, before the paper. In this case, however, I didn't want to leave Cathy with so much paper in mass confusion. And, I knew Cathy could handle organizing the supplies. So, we tackled the paper.

We had at least four or five bins and boxes of paper staring at us. The volume alone was daunting. Cathy looked at me for direction. Where to start? With the big stuff, of course!

Yes, there's even big stuff within boxes of paper. I dug through the boxes, pulling out big chunks of paper – the magazines, envelopes of photos, chunks of paper stapled together, and sorted the chunks by big categories: financial papers, kid papers, photos, magazines, catalogs, writing projects and so on. I worked hard to reduce the number of boxes of paper so Cathy could see real progress. I wanted to create enough positive energy in the form of relief and order, to keep her motivated and optimistic about the project. By the time we finished that day, we had reduced four boxes to two, and had identified a number of general categories. Cathy was thrilled with the results, and I was relieved to have been able to transform a chaotic, overwhelming space, into an appealing environment with potential to be a truly functional space.

When I returned to Cathy's office a week later, she had begun to sort by focusing on the box with the greater quantity of "big stuff." In this case, one box had numerous old file folders that had to be examined. Their contents had been combined with more recent papers. We worked our way from the file folders to chunks of paper and finally to individual pieces of paper. It was only after we finished sorting most of the papers that I began creating new files to hold the paper that would remain in the office.

Had we started with individual pieces of paper, it's likely that it would have taken four to six times longer to do, if it got done at all. It's also very unlikely that I would have been asked back again for further help. As it was, after four hours of work together, Cathy had a box of newly labeled files and most of the paper had been sorted and put away.

When you first silence the negative energy of the paper by pulling it all together, dealing with big stuff first, you too can make significant progress. When you make significant progress you'll feel such relief and pride that you'll want to continue working.

This process won't make dealing with paper quick, fun or easy. Organizing and clearing paper is hard and time consuming, even when you know how to tackle it. But, if you eliminate the negative energy first and raise the positive energy by organizing big items, you are more likely to be successful. Think of paper clearing as an energy challenge. If you can handle paper, you can clear anything.

Letting Go

Not long ago I found a baby blue jay with a broken wing. He tried so hard to fly away from me, but alas, his wounded wing dragged him down. My little dog, Jake, thought the bird would make a tasty snack, and I really had to scramble to keep him from grabbing the frightened little bird.

After a scuffle, I managed to get Jake into the house. Then I went back to move the bird to a safer spot. I knew he would probably die, but I didn't want him to die in terror from an attack by Jake. When I bent down to pull him from the azalea bush where he was hiding, I found his wounded wing tangled up in the brush. There was no way he could move forward to get away from me. I untangled him and carefully placed him outside our yard under a large bush where he would be better hidden and could die more peacefully.

One day when I was standing in my kitchen window looking at that large bush, wistfully remembering the plight of the blue jay, it occurred to me that the little bird is like many people who have trouble parting with their stuff. They see their belongings as treasures that they couldn't possibly part with, but they don't realize exactly how those things really weigh them down.

Their belongings function like the wounded wing of the bird. When the wing was broken, it no longer served the bird. It only held him back from making progress toward safety. The "stuff" you hold onto that you no longer love or use holds you back because it distracts you, makes you feel overwhelmed by its volume and the decisions to be made, and keeps you from getting clear about what really does matter. You cannot make easy progress and fully thrive in your life until you let go of the things that are weighing you down.

Chapter Thirteen

Maintenance

Clearing clutter is an important first step to creating a space that has a positive effect on your performance. Unfortunately, clearing clutter is a process, not an event. Once a space has been cleared, daily effort is needed to keep it clear and maintain the positive energy that the initial clutter clearing had created.

Clear As You Go

It happened again today! I was looking for a recipe and ran into a paper pile that wasn't even on my radar. I keep special recipes with the phone books on the shelf of a telephone table in the kitchen. As is my habit, when I reached for the recipe folder I also took a look at all the other items on the shelf. Not only did I rediscover an excellent, healthy eating cookbook, but I also found several out of date phone directories and guides to exploring Richmond, a spiral binder and a loose-leaf binder that could be emptied. I felt good when I saw that stack of miscellaneous items shrink, and I was rewarded with the find of a great cookbook I had forgotten about.

Remember, you too can regularly experience the pleasure of purging if you do it as you go about your every day activities! It only takes seconds to pitch a few things, and the benefits far outweigh the effort. Every time you get rid of something, you are creating clarity for yourself and clearing a path to more prosperity.

"I'm Going Backwards!"

"I think I'm going backwards," Sally said. "I'm getting piles of stuff everywhere again!" I took a look around, and sure enough, piles of clutter were creeping across both the upper and lower counters in her kitchen, areas we'd tackled and conquered at least two years before. Cookbooks were piled on her table, an unfinished project. The biggest pile could be seen from the front door, a pile of things intended for sale on eBay® and destinations elsewhere.

"Sally, all it takes is one pile to create a negative spin energetically. Like attracts like. One pile attracts others. The first is the bud of other piles. One pile gave you and the space permission to sprout other piles!" I said.

I had a hunch it was the big "eBay" pile that started the spin. When I suggested that to Sally, she agreed. "That's where it all started!"

You really cannot afford to have any highly visible pockets of negative energy, like piles of clutter. If you do, you are fighting an uphill battle. Like attracts like. Wouldn't you rather attract calmness and peace? Clear those piles and clutter puddles and feel yourself relax! It's a great investment of time and energy!

Clear Clutter Every Day to Keep Your Life Moving!

I can hear your thoughts. They go like this, "How can I possibly clear clutter every day? I have too much to do. There's just no way!"

I'm not talking about tackling an attic, a closet or even a drawer. I'm talking about clearing clutter in areas that you touch every day. Here are some examples.

- Junk mail
- Email messages
- Voicemail messages
- Clothes that don't fit when you put them on
- Shoes that feel uncomfortable when you put them on
- Papers you find when you look for something in a drawer
- Snack wrappers
- Odd scraps of paper
- Broken things that you don't intend to repair

Look for clutter at all times! Take pleasure in eliminating it ***immediately!*** Don't put it off! Give yourself the chance to experience the light feeling and the satisfaction that come from having fewer things bugging you. And, enjoy being able to find things more easily because you have fewer hiding places!

Making Changes Too Quickly

It's quite common for my students to get all revved up to clear, clear, clear when they learn that clutter is a source of negative energy and a major block to getting what you want in life. They tell me that they can't wait to get home and get to work. They wish it was already the weekend so they could start immediately.

It's actually a good thing that they have a day or two before they can get to work clearing clutter. When you clear things from any part of your home or office you are shifting energies. Because everything is connected, those shifts affect everything in your life. When energies are shifted too quickly, life can get chaotic or you could get sick. It's best to do some clearing, then take a break of several days to let energies settle.

I am living proof that clearing too quickly has some risks. When I returned from my first full week of feng shui training I was excited about feng shui and motivated to make some major changes in my home. I moved my office from an upstairs bedroom to a downstairs sitting room. That was a major change! We did it in a day. Soon after that, I got sick with a cold.

A client of mine came away from her first class and began clearing her whole house plus an attached garage. Shortly after she completed all that work, she called me and said many things were breaking. That's the kind of chaos that can happen when clearing happens too quickly.

It's best to clear in a slow, deliberate manner instead of doing too much too fast. Pace yourself, and allow time for energies to settle. Then you can keep going without disrupting your life too much!

Maintenance: A Permanent Commitment

Just when you think that you've cleared out every nook and cranny in your home, garage and car, you find something else to that needs attention! It really is a never ending chore to keep clear and current with your space.

So, how do you keep up with it? I like to take advantage of every opportunity to clear that presents itself in my daily activities. For example, I had to pull everything out of my car to move some furniture: the seats, all of my organizing supplies, my CD collection, books and other miscellaneous items I thought I needed in the car. Rather than just haul it all back in without a glance, as I have done many times before, this time I made the decision that I wanted fewer things in my car. I went through the various containers and "got real" about what I actually use. Some things went to the attic because I occasionally use them when we travel. Some things went to the shed. Other things went to my office and the kitchen. And, a few things went into the trash! I ended up with half as many things to haul back out to my car. Victory!

The next time you find yourself pawing through a cluttered drawer, take a moment to clear it out. If you don't have time to tackle the whole project, look for a few items to throw away or move to a better location. Every effort of clearing and creating order helps you maintain your commitment to a clutter free life. The end result will be a clutter free mind and a life of true happiness and abundance. So, keep on clearing!

Goals for Creating High Performance Environments

1. Create a high energy space. Have only those things that have positive energy, things that you love or use.
2. Eliminate things that have a dead or negative energy. Lose them!
3. Have only the quantity of things that feel comfortable in the space.
4. Make a commitment to regularly tend and clear your space to keep its energy high.

Chapter Fourteen

Do It! It Works!

You may be thinking, "This is interesting. It makes sense. But, it's a lot of work. What if I spend precious time and energy clearing and setting up my space and nothing changes for the better? Will doing this really produce results?"

Over and over again I've seen clients' lives improve after clearing clutter and setting up their homes and offices so they are organized and utterly comfortable. A number of them moved on to new work, new relationships and even new homes. Before clearing clutter they floated along in a sea of confusion caused by the confusion in their environments. Then they changed the energy of their environments and became more intentional in their decision-making, more productive in their actions, and more successful in their lives.

Think of Martin who quadrupled his income. Remember Betty whose newly organized home and office set the stage for a new relationship. And don't forget Dave who regained his confidence when he put the legs back on his sofa and moved his furniture into "power positions."

What About You?

What do you really want? What you have in your space and how it's arranged affects what happens in your work and in your life. Is what you're holding onto holding you back? There are many things you have no control of – the economy, the behavior of others, the weather – but you do have the ability to affect the condition of the spaces in which you work and live.

Becoming conscious of the effect of environment on performance is the first step. Becoming committed to regularly clearing clutter and creating spaces of color and light and positive energy is the next. It's an on-going step. As your life changes, so too should your spaces. Think of them as an outer skin, a reflection of your inner self. With constant tending and maintenance you can create spaces that support optimal performance and success in creating the life you really want.

You can create spaces that support optimal performance and success in creating the life you really want.

About the Author

Debbie Bowie is an engaging speaker, a highly effective feng shui practitioner, and a gets-things-done professional organizer. She established her organizing business in 1998. Helping clients clear, organize and decorate their homes and offices has allowed Debbie to observe the impact that such improvements have on her clients' lives and work.

One of Debbie's passions is to understand relationships. Her deep understanding of the nature of relationships equips her to give poignant presentations that often touch people personally and spur them to action. This understanding also enables her to facilitate highly effective feng shui and organizing consultations.

Debbie's formal training includes a B.A. an M.A. in Art History, an M.S. in Counseling. She has also had training in Pyramid School Feng Shui, Black Hat Sect Feng Shui, and is a graduate of the Western School of Feng Shui™. In 2007, Debbie was one of an inaugural group of professional organizers to receive the designation of Certified Professional Organizer®.

Book Debbie to speak at your next meeting or event.

"Wow--what an exciting, entertaining and educational speaker! Debbie spoke to our Women's Club and immediately engaged everyone with her practical and realistic approach. It felt as if she had already seen the "mess" we were all hiding at home or office, or at the very least, could read our minds. Her direct approach, couched in a great sense of humor, immediately put everyone at ease. With her calm energy motivating all of us, we felt empowered to get moving and put her easy steps to clearing clutter in effect ASAP to create that positive living/work environment. I can't wait for next month's meeting to hear what everyone accomplished!!"

Janet Bagnall, President
Women of Meadowbrook Country Club, Inc.

Clear Clutter, Improve Your Physical Environment and Watch Your Performance Soar!

Debbie conducts keynotes and breakout sessions for organizations that want to create high performance work environments that set the stage for employees to be more organized, have more clarity, have more energy and be more productive. Debbie doesn't waste time on platitudes and theories. In her engaging and humorous style she gives real life ideas to produce immediate results. Depending on your format, time available and meeting objectives, her speeches can run from thirty minutes to three hours.

For availability and booking information, you can reach Debbie at 804-730-4991.

www.rockscissorspaperinstitute.com

Final Thoughts

1. Share *Rock Scissors Paper: Understanding How Environment Affects Your Behavior on a Daily Basis* with your friends, family members and colleagues. Buy 50 copies and receive a 25% discount off the retail price. Call 804-730-4991 for special pricing on larger quantities.

2. Please share stories of your challenges and successes, and any comments you have about how this book has helped you. Mail or send an email to:

Debbie Bowie
Rock Scissors Paper Institute
7293 Jay Way
Mechanicsville, VA 23111
debbie@rockscissorspaperinstitute.com

3. Go to Debbie's blog at www.rockscissorspaperinstitute.com for more information about how environment affects performance and ideas about how to be more productive, gain more clarity, have more energy and feel more in control of your life.